"A great deal of professional attention is rightly given to the physical health of people with profound and multiple learning disabilities. As much should be given to their mental health and wellbeing. Afterall, physical health makes life possible, mental health makes it feel worth living! The drawing of information from research and real life mean this book is both informative and practical. Andrew and Julie's insights act as a powerful enabler for the kind of reflective practice that will create better lives for people to live."

Jo Grace, sensory engagement and inclusion specialist

"[This book] hits a mark seldom achieved, in not only posing questions related to the position of children, young people and adults with profound and multiple learning difficulties in 21st century society, but also in finding some answers. The book opens with a discussion of current practice, and then explodes into life with the results of a fascinating and wide-ranging international questionnaire which takes in the thoughts of practitioners in 20 different countries. Finally, the authors explore what is possible in one truly outstanding UK educational provision, given the funding. This is a thought provoking and innovative study, and I commend it to you."

Peter Imray, freelance trainer, advisor and writer on SEND

"The book... is a very useful read for practitioners working with people with PMLD of all ages across the world. With a great number of quotes from professionals working in educational settings and other provisions in the UK but also in 19 other countries this book feels like hearing their voice, getting to know their practice and learning from them. The whole book but especially the third part of it, which describes in detail the exceptional example of Chailey Heritage School (specific filled in profiles are provided) is going to benefit immensely everyone who would like hands-on advice on how to improve the well-being and independence of people with PMLD. The authors have also drawn throughout the book links between research, policy and practice which makes their work of interest to researchers in the field too."

Lila Kossyvaki, Lecturer in Severe Profound and Multiple Learning Disabilities

Enhancing Wellbeing and Independence for Young People with Profound and Multiple Learning Difficulties

This unique resource book explores what wellbeing, community participation and independence mean for young people with profound and multiple learning difficulties (PMLD). Bringing together results of an extensive survey of more than 100 schools that teach young people with PMLD, the authors present many innovative ways in which schools are working to ensure young people with PMLD have lives of value that are as rich and meaningful as possible.

Organised into three cohesive parts, this book provides a comprehensive insight into established theories and current perspectives on wellbeing and independence for people with PMLD before exploring the results from the *Lives Lived Well* survey and other international research, and then it helpfully illustrates best practice in action with a close look at an established, very successful specialist school.

This book can be used as a guide, resource and inspiration for adults sharing their lives with young people with PMLD – whether practitioners or parents – and concludes by asking what we can learn from these young people to support us all in living life to the fullest.

Andrew Colley is former Senior Lecturer in Special Education at the University of East London, UK. He has master's degrees in special education from the Universities of Birmingham and Cambridge and has taught young people with profound and multiple learning difficulties at schools in Essex and Cambridgeshire.

Julie Tilbury is Lead Teacher for children with profound and multiple learning difficulties at Chailey Heritage School in East Sussex, UK, and has worked in special schools for 30 years. She has a master's degree in special education from the University of Birmingham and is studying for an EdD at the University of Buckingham.

Enhancing Wellbeing and Independence for Young People with Profound and Multiple Learning Difficulties

Lives Lived Well

Andrew Colley and Julie Tilbury
with Simon Yates

LONDON AND NEW YORK

First edition published 2022
by Routledge
2 Park Square, Milton Park, Abingdon, Oxon, OX14 4RN

and by Routledge
605 Third Avenue, New York, NY 10158

Routledge is an imprint of the Taylor & Francis Group, an informa business

© 2022 Andrew Colley and Julie Tilbury

The right of Andrew Colley and Julie Tilbury to be identified as authors of this work has been asserted by them in accordance with sections 77 and 78 of the Copyright, Designs and Patents Act 1988.

All rights reserved. No part of this book may be reprinted or reproduced or utilised in any form or by any electronic, mechanical, or other means, now known or hereafter invented, including photocopying and recording, or in any information storage or retrieval system, without permission in writing from the publishers.

Trademark notice: Product or corporate names may be trademarks or registered trademarks, and are used only for identification and explanation without intent to infringe.

British Library Cataloguing-in-Publication Data
A catalogue record for this book is available from the British Library

Library of Congress Cataloging-in-Publication Data
Names: Colley, Andrew (Teacher), author. | Tilbury, Julie, author.
Title: Enhancing wellbeing and independence for young people with
    profound and multiple learning difficulties : lives lived well / Andrew
    Colley and Julie Tilbury ; with Simon Yates.
Description: Abingdon, Oxon ; New York, NY : Routledge, 2022. |
    Includes bibliographical references and index.
Identifiers: LCCN 2021014596 (print) | LCCN 2021014597 (ebook) |
    ISBN 9780367564155 (hardback) | ISBN 9780367564063 (paperback) |
    ISBN 9781003097648 (ebook)
Subjects: LCSH: Learning disabled children—Education. | Learning
    disabled children—Mental health. | Special education—Psychological
    aspects. | Autonomy (Psychology) | Well-being. | Chailey Heritage
    School. | Special education—Great Britain.
Classification: LCC LC4704 .C629 2022 (print) | LCC LC4704 (ebook) |
    DDC 371.9—dc23
LC record available at https://lccn.loc.gov/2021014596
LC ebook record available at https://lccn.loc.gov/2021014597

ISBN: 978-0-367-56415-5 (hbk)
ISBN: 978-0-367-56406-3 (pbk)
ISBN: 978-1-003-09764-8 (ebk)

DOI: 10.4324/9781003097648

Typeset in Melior
by Apex CoVantage, LLC

Contents

Acknowledgements	ix
1 Introduction	1
Part I	**7**
2 What do we mean by wellbeing?	9
3 What do we mean by independence?	20
4 Wellbeing and independence in international and UK national policy	28
Part II	**43**
5 An introduction to the *Lives Lived Well* surveys	45
6 The *Lives Lived Well* surveys: wellbeing	50
7 The *Lives Lived Well* surveys: independence	76
8 The *Lives Lived Well* surveys: wellbeing and independence beyond school	105
9 The *Lives Lived Well* surveys: the link between policy and practice	121

viii Contents

Part III

Focus on Chailey Heritage School   **131**

10   Welcome to Chailey Heritage School!   133

11   Supporting wellbeing at Chailey Heritage School   143

12   Supporting independence at Chailey Heritage School   173

13   Conclusion   187

The *Lives Lived Well* UK questionnaire   190

The *Lives Lived Well* international questionnaire   203

Index   211

Acknowledgements

We would like to thank all the young people from Chailey Heritage School whose photos appear in this book and everybody who completed the *Lives Lived Well* UK and International surveys. In particular, we owe a special thank-you to the following:

David Bliss
Cambridge University Faculty of Education
Lucía Días Carcelén
Helen Dunman
María Carrasco Galdó
Peter Imray
Ruth Kershner
Bea Maes
Penny Lacey
Prithvi Perepa
Gena Tan Li Xin
Jimson Tham
Simon Yates

Introduction

Welcome to *Enhancing Wellbeing and Independence for Young People with Profound and Multiple Learning Difficulties: Lives Lived Well*! Written largely during the global COVID-19 pandemic and successive UK lockdowns, we hope that in many ways this will be a practical and 'feel-good' book for anyone who works or is in other ways involved with young people with profound and multiple learning difficulties (PMLD), in or out of school: 'feel good' because it is principally a way of showcasing good practice with learners with PMLD in schools and other provision all around the world. We hear some wonderfully positive voices telling us about how they support their students to be physically comfortable and emotionally happy, as well as to be and feel as independent as possible, and we also hear how schools facilitate these young people's participation in the wider community. There is truly something for everyone to learn here, whether it be the way one school in the UK encourages its pupils with PMLD to listen to the sound of Shakespeare or how in Cyprus everyone benefits from as much outdoor activity in the Mediterranean sun as they possibly can!

Let's start though by defining what we mean by 'PMLD'. For a book which, as we shall see, has had such a large input from around the world and is also aimed at both an international and UK audience, we find ourselves agreeing with Nind and Strnadova (2020) that we 'cannot supply a universally agreed definition of profound intellectual and multiple disabilities (as none exists)' (p. 1). Even the terms used to describe this group can be different from country to country and can be educationally or medically based or a combination of the two. In the UK and for the purposes of this book, we use PMLD, although

DOI: 10.4324/9781003097648-1

a lot of other countries favour 'profound intellectual and multiple disabilities' (PIMD), whilst in France, which we will hear from in Part II, 'polyhandicap' is the 'mot du jour' but doesn't maybe translate so well literally into English.

We must though at least try to explain at the outset, what some of the defining characteristics might be of the group this book is about whilst, of course, never forgetting that they are, in fact, not a group at all but very much individuals in their own right. This is a fact which is deeply embedded in the approach used at Chailey Heritage School, in Sussex in the UK, which we devote Part III to. We know for instance (DfE, 2020) that there may be about 11,000 learners with PMLD in English schools. There will also, of course, be many more than 11,000 different needs, profiles, strengths, weaknesses, diagnoses, conditions, personalities, means of communication and so on. The list which marks each one out as unique is, in fact, endless.

Definitions have been put forward, amongst others, by the UK Department for Education (DfE) in 2012; Imray and Colley (2017) in *Inclusion is Dead: Long Live Inclusion!* (London: Routledge) and by Nind and Strnadova (2020) in *Belonging for People With Profound Intellectual and Multiple Disabilities* (London: Routledge). Summarising these and other definitions we can perhaps agree that pupils with PMLD can have most or all of the following characteristics:

- Very severe learning difficulties
- Sensory impairments
- Physical disabilities
- Complex medical conditions
- Behaviours which sometimes challenge those around them

In addition, they are likely to communicate in unconventional or idiosyncratic ways but can communicate through gestures, body language, sounds, eye pointing and occasionally the use of simple symbolic communication systems such as the Picture Exchange Communication System (PECS) as described by Bondy and Frost (2001), although as we discuss in Chapter 7, PECS can be overused with this group of learners and is generally inappropriate. Finally, and crucially for this book where we discuss independence, these young people will require high levels of adult support throughout their lives.

In the UK, these young people tend, in the main, to go to special schools and the raw data provided by the DfE School Census Statistics Team in its Get Information About Schools tool (https://get-information-schools.service.gov.uk/) backs that up. Internationally, the picture is much more varied, and as we find out in Part II, whilst many do attend special schools, others are often placed in mainstream schools or in residential provision. In some countries, we have found, there is very little, if any, provision at all.

The book is structured in three parts

Part I is based on an extensive search of literature around the wellbeing, community participation and independence of learners with PMLD carried out in 2020 by Andrew Colley as part of a Master's by Research with the Cambridge University Faculty of Education. This part of the book discusses how researchers and other writers have sought to define and frame wellbeing and independence for this group. It also examines how international and UK policy has defined these terms, showing that, very often, policy excludes young people with PMLD.

Part II presents the data from the two *Lives Lived Well* surveys, the first of which was distributed to schools in the UK as part of the same research project and the second was provided internationally to practitioners working with young people with PMLD specifically for this book. The surveys asked teachers and other practitioners how their school, or schools in their country, enhance the wellbeing and independence of this group of learners and about the barriers they face to community participation. It also asks whether they felt that education policy in their countries takes account sufficiently of learners with PMLD. Fifty-two UK schools responded to the survey, and there were 66 responses to the international survey from 19 different countries.

In **Part III**, we visit Chailey Heritage School in Sussex in the UK and are given a vivid and practice-based account of how it enhances the wellbeing of its learners on a day-to-day basis as well as how it supports them to be as independent as possible and participate fully in the wider community.

4 Introduction

At its heart, the book shows clearly that, if done well, teaching young people with PMLD is one of the most demanding but also rewarding jobs a teacher can do, that those who do work with this group around the world do so because they are committed to ensuring that these young people are healthy and happy, are as independent as possible and have as much access to the wider community and opportunities as their peers who do not have learning difficulties. We say this because in many countries, there can be a hierarchy of teaching which places the teaching of academic subjects to a minority of gifted and talented pupils at the top, but we happily challenge that in this book and show that, in fact, teaching young people with PMLD demands the greatest skill, reflection, hard work and dedication from the teachers, classroom assistants and a myriad of other professionals who work around, and with, each young person.

The book is also timely, with lockdowns around the world impacting significantly on the more vulnerable members of society, especially when carers have not been able to visit, planning has stopped and services have not been provided. This has not only left people with PMLD unsupported but has also had an impact on their behaviour and mental health as well as on the health of parents and carers, often exacerbating existing issues.

There has arguably been a lack of research (Ware, 2017) into the education of pupils with PMLD and even less which focuses specifically on their wellbeing and independence. So we hope that in many ways, this book will, at least in part, begin to look into these issues in some depth. It will also present a broad knowledge base which all practitioners around the world can access so that wherever they are around the globe we can say that people with PMLD are given the chance to live their lives well. . . .

Reference list

Bondy, A., & Frost, L. (2001). The picture exchange communication system. *Behavior Modification, 25*(5), 725–744.

DfE. (2020a). *Special educational needs in England.* Retrieved from www.gov.uk/government/statistics/special-educational-needs-in-england-january-2020

DfE. (2020b). *Get information about schools.* Retrieved from https://get-infor mation-schools.service.gov.uk/

Imray, P., & Colley, A. (2017). *Inclusion is dead: Long live inclusion!* London: Routledge.

Nind, M., & Strnadova, I. (Eds.). (2020). *Belonging for people with profound intellectual and multiple disabilities* (pp. 1–21). London: Routledge.

Ware, J. (2017, September). *Assessment for learners with PMLD.* Paper presented at BERA Annual Conference, Brighton.

PART I

What do we mean by wellbeing?

What is wellbeing?

So what have writers and researchers found about what that term we hear so much these days, 'wellbeing', means when applied to people with profound and multiple learning difficulties (PMLD)?

As mentioned in the introduction to this book, there has arguably been a lack of research (Ware, 2017) into the education of pupils with PMLD, and even less which focuses specifically on the wellbeing of this group (Schuller & Watson, 2009). An online library search carried out by one of the authors using the University of Cambridge *iDiscover* database revealed very few books or journal articles which contain either in their subject or title the term *wellbeing* combined with key words such as *profound* or *complex*, although in 2012, the *Journal of Student Wellbeing* published an article by Lyons and Cassebohm called 'Student Wellbeing for Those With Profound Intellectual and Multiple Disabilities (PIMD): Same, or Same but Different?' In this article, the authors respond to the Australian curriculum for all by outlining a grounded theory of subjective wellbeing as applied to learners with PIMD and conclude that while their atypical communication means it is not always possible to assess their subjective wellbeing, it is possible to assess their happiness and measure their quality of life. More recently, Maes, Penne, Vastmans and Arthur-Kelley (2020) call for a recognition that education for this group must always be seen from the perspective of quality of life and emotional wellbeing.

10 Part I

A small amount of literature explores issues around the wellbeing of young people with all learning difficulties and of that some sources focus on young people with severe learning difficulties (SLD), although as we and other practitioners know, young people with SLD do not display the same learning differences as those with PMLD (Imray & Colley, 2017) and are not always even in the same class or group in a UK special school for instance.

This research gap makes it difficult to find a definition of *wellbeing* which is applicable to young people with PMLD. A recent book by Fox, Laverty and Chowdhury (2020) is described in its forward as a "resource for helping children with severe and complex needs" (p. xvii), but the authors do acknowledge that "most policy and research is based on pupils in mainstream schools" (p. 15). The authors use the following definition of the term *wellbeing* from the National Children's Bureau which is essentially applicable to all children:

> a sense of optimism, confidence, happiness, clarity, vitality, self-worth, achievement, having a meaning and purpose, engagement and satisfying relationships with others and understanding oneself, and responding effectively to one's emotions.
>
> (Weare, 2015, p. 3)

This definition, however, is not so easy to apply to young people with PMLD who, as we know, may not be able to communicate in ways which would allow their communication partners to be certain that they are expressing a sense of their own 'optimism' or 'self-worth', let alone that the young people themselves are able to respond effectively to their own emotions, although teachers and others may be able to make relatively reliable judgements as to whether or not they are happy. Even this though can be a challenge. Angelman Syndrome, for instance, is a "genetic condition that causes severe physical and learning disabilities . . . a person with Angelman syndrome will need support throughout their life" (NHS, 2020), and in many cases, a young person with this condition may fit the criteria for having PMLD as outlined in Chapter 1, and the authors and many others reading this book will probably have known or taught someone with Angelman syndrome in a class of other pupils identified as having PMLD. One of the features of Angelman syndrome can be that the young person appears to be smiling and therefore is assumed to be happy which may mask the fact that they are not happy at all, and in fact, one of the authors of this book taught a girl with Angelman syndrome and no one noticed for many months that she must have been in terrible pain from several broken teeth! Simmons and Watson (2014), in their excellent book *The PMLD Ambiguity* (2014), point out that many children with PMLD may have learnt to live with a certain amount of pain simply because despite our best intentions we are still expecting them to express that pain in conventional ways.

For a more specialised definition of wellbeing, the National Association of Independent and Non-Maintained Special Schools (NASS) brings together wellbeing and mental health in one definition:

> Mental Health is a positive sense of wellbeing which enables an individual to function in society and meet the demands of everyday life.
>
> (NASS, 2017, p. 5)

Here again, making reliable judgements about the mental health of a young person with PMLD is not always easy (Rose, Hawley, Fergusson, & Jament, 2009), especially when a young person does not communicate in a conventional way, and Rose, Hawley, Fergusson and Jament identify a further area of concern for many professionals working in this field: the challenges of distinguishing between features of a learning difficulty and possible indicators of mental health problems. In other words, to what extent is it possible to identify a mental health condition which is not a manifestation of the primary diagnosis, whatever that may be? Diagnosing and treating anyone for a mental health issue is also, of course, usually based on a conversational exchange (Bouras, Hardy, & Holt, 2011), often called 'talking therapy', and is, in addition, culture-bound to a certain extent. Symptoms and behaviours are interpreted by professionals and compared against cultural and linguistic norms, and here again, when that person has complex learning needs and unconventional communication pathways, these therapeutic exchanges do not often, if ever, work as they might for the rest of us.

Other definitions of *wellbeing* in the literature of special education may be more appropriate for young people with PMLD, although here again, they are framed around a wide spectrum of learning difficulties and differences. Carpenter et al. (2015), when discussing young people with complex learning difficulties and disabilities, find that wellbeing can be emotional, psychological and social, and Dee, Byers, Hayhoe and Maudslay (2002) mention feelings of personal worth and contentment.

The Capabilities Approach first defined by economist Amartya Sen (1999) has been developed by American philosopher Martha Nussbaum (2007) as a way of acknowledging the capabilities of people with learning difficulties. Of Nussbaum's 10 "Central Human Capabilities" (2007, p. 76) the first two in particular can perhaps help us to define wellbeing for people with PMLD:

1   Life: being able to live to the end of a life of normal length.
2   Bodily health: being able to have good health.

Exploring these key capabilities further with respect to people with learning difficulties and disability, Nussbaum emphasises that people should be able to live "a life compatible with human dignity" (p. 79), be "active in the world" (p. 73), have diverse "opportunities for activity" (p. 74), enjoy nature and experience "life, health and bodily integrity as well as emotional attachments and the removal of overwhelming fear and anxiety" (p. 168). As we will see however, when we discuss community participation in more depth later, opportunities for forming emotional attachments can be limited for someone with very profound needs.

Moving beyond simple definitions, however, to what extent do researchers and other writers show that people with PMLD are able consistently to achieve the same level of wellbeing as everyone else and, in particular, their peers with mild to moderate learning difficulties? Here again, it is difficult to find research which specifically focuses on profound or complex needs. Grant, Goward, Richardson and Ramcharan (2010) and O'Brien (2016) have shown that people with all learning difficulties are more likely to experience living circumstances and life events associated with an increased risk of mental and physical health problems as well as financial constraints, and those with PMLD are more likely to experience poverty (BOND, 2013). Rates of mental illness are considerably higher for those with all learning difficulties than in the general population (Bouras et al., 2011), and although it is again difficult to isolate statistics for people with PMLD, Bradley, Summers, Wood and Bryson (2004) found a significant increase in symptoms of mental illness using the Diagnostic Assessment for the Severely Handicapped (Matson, Gardner, Coe, & Sovner, 1991) criteria in young people with autism and severe intellectual disability compared to those with autism alone.

To conclude then this discussion about what writers and researchers have said about what wellbeing actually looks like for someone with PMLD, Johnson and Walmsley (2010) in their fascinating book *People With Intellectual Disabilities. Towards a Good Life?* pick up on this key word *dignity* and are concerned that people with PMLD risk living unfulfilled lives and that we are still failing to ensure they have "a life compatible with human dignity" (Nussbaum, 2007 p. 79), with the lives of their parents and carers often consisting mainly of "mundane care routines punctuated by painful memories" (Simmons & Watson, 2014. p. 8). To what extent schools have also identified these issues and how they seek to address them in their everyday practice were key themes in the *Lives Lived Well* surveys, and we look at how teachers and practitioners do this in Part II.

Community participation and wellbeing

Many of the definitions of wellbeing explored in this chapter include relationships and functioning in society as key indicators of wellbeing for all people, including those with learning difficulties, and interactions within communities of all types have been shown (Nijs, Vlaskamp, & Maes, 2016) to be supportive of developmental and quality-of-life outcomes, with Nind and Strnadova (2020) going so far as to call community participation fundamental not just to quality of life but also to our "final landscape of inclusion" (p. 11). So, again, what does the literature of special education tell us about community participation for this group as a contributory factor to their wellbeing?

De Haas (2020) undertook a literature search and found very little research around relationship and community participation for people with PMLD. However it is possible to identify a number of attempts in recent literature to define what is meant by 'community participation' for people with special educational needs and disabilities, although again these definitions are restricted to a certain extent to people with mild, moderate or severe learning difficulties rather than specifically for those with PMLD whose needs and circumstances may have significant implications for their community participation.

Hoskin (2018) in writing specifically about young people with Duchenne muscular dystrophy (DMD) defines community participation as being "about friends, engaging in local activities, getting out and about, joining clubs" (p. 143). Although young people with DMD do not by any means all also have profound learning difficulties, her definition is one which could be applied to this cohort. Johnson and Walmsley (2010) also place the emphasis firmly on social ties as well as the "relationships people with disabilities may want or need to lead good lives" (p. 135), but De Haas (2020) reminds us that accessing meaningful leisure activities with friends has always been a problem for those with PMLD. Bellamy, Croot, Bush, Berry and Smith (2010) found that parents and carers of children with PMLD preferred definitions which highlight "the circumstances which are necessary to enable individuals with PMLD to be given the opportunity to participate in their immediate situation, their community and ultimately in wider society" (p. 232).

This emphasis on relationship as community is echoed by Nussbaum (2007, p. 78) in that list of central human capabilities we referred to earlier with two further of those capabilities being

5   Emotions: being able to have attachments to things and people
7   Affiliation: being able to live with and towards others

The quality and shape of social networks are central to the wellbeing of us all (Taylor, 2014), and at the time of writing this book, all over the world, people are suffering from losing out on those social networks in the COVID-19 lockdowns. Historically, of course, and very unjustly, many people with learning difficulties only had restricted access to social networks anyway. These restrictions were originally established in the UK by the 1899 Elementary Education (Defective and Epileptic Children) Act (56 / 57 Vict. C42). Only children "not being imbecile" (p. 11) would receive education and decisions of selection would be made by medical practitioners. Those we describe now as having PMLD were routinely institutionalised in the large asylums, which were built around the same time (Frogley & Welch, 1993), or were kept at home. Even with the advent of community care in the last decades of the 20th century (Shakespeare, 2014), the general fragmentation of social and family ties meant that most disabled people began to live in the community "just as the concept of community has been eroded" (p. 195), and Johnson and Walmsley (2010) remind us that "over a quarter of a century after the discrediting and closure of segregated institutions, there is not a great deal of evidence that policies premised on community inclusion deliver a good enough life" (p. 96). Many families with a disabled member risk living isolated lives, and there is the constant danger that these young people may end up simply being "present in the community but not participating in it" (Shakespeare, 2014, p. 193). It has also been shown that socially isolated people die at two or three times the rate of people "with a network of social relationships and sources of emotional support" (ibid., p. 189), with people with PMLD (Glover & Ayub, 2010) dying on average 24 years earlier than the rest of the population.

The community of someone with PMLD is, with a certain inevitability then, largely focused on their parents and siblings (Nijs et al., 2016), their school and others who provide care and assistance. Nijs (2020) categorises these types of relationships as 'hierarchical': parents as well as teachers, and 'horizontal': classmates and siblings. All these types of relationship can, however, be valid and meaningful micro-communities for the young person, and Shakespeare (2014) points out that personal assistance and care is in itself a relationship and that those who provide it, whether family members or outside agencies, can provide a young person with a valuable community life. As for communities of disabled people or advocacy groups which have become more prevalent in recent decades, Hanisch (2014) asks whether given the high level of need and the atypical communication of this group, is this realistic for those with PMLD?

Nevertheless, the incidence of people with PMLD in a community is so low (De Haas, 2020) that other people may have no or limited experience of them. Even in communities and environments such as schools and clubs in which people with PMLD are together with non-disabled or typically developing peers, fully participating can be elusive. Prudhomme, Geiger, Luger, and Bullen (2018) worked in centres in South Africa where young people with PMLD were amongst the client group. One of their key observations was that visitors to the centres were often "overwhelmed by the clients with PIMD" (p. 4) and did not seem to know how to interact with them, often migrating towards interacting with the more physically able and communicative children and adults. Similarly, Kamstra, van der Putten and Vlaskamp (2015) find that where persons with PMLD participate in inclusive settings in which they can meet typically developing peers, interactions amongst and between those typically developing peers (Nijs, Vlaskamp, & Maes, 2016) tend to be more frequent than interactions between those typically developing peers and pupils with PMLD, and Lacey and Scull (2015) found that even in fully inclusive school settings, lesson time can simply consist of keeping a learner with PMLD visibly busy with no real connection to the rest of the class or, in some more extreme cases, the learner is simply taken out of the room so as not to disrupt the learning of their peers.

The full community participation of learners with PMLD can then be problematic, and as a consequence have a negative impact on their wellbeing, although Simmons and Watson (2014) suggest again that Nussbaum's Capabilities Approach attempts to redefine what is meant by the participation of disabled learners in society in a way which acknowledges the reality of their lived experience. Equality, Nussbaum (2007) reminds us, should mean more than just access to buildings, transport and schools and should be about living in communities which are so diverse that we can all learn from each other. Community participation, according to Nussbaum, should be about "protecting pluralism" (p. 79) and valuing humanity in all its diversity. Simmons and Watson (2014) point out that for this to be achieved society would need to adopt an "alternative lens of disability" (p. 18) and a "repositioning of profoundly disabled people that reveals their social and cultural engagement in the world and allows for their personhood to emerge" (p. 16). More recently, Nind and Strnadova (2020) suggest that perhaps we need to adopt a more accessible and nuanced definition of *community* for this group to include feeling comfortable and being understood and that *belonging* as a term may be preferable to *community* because it is about place, memory, relationships and having friends with similar experiences including the experience of having a disability.

In Part II, we show how schools the world over are responding to the challenges of enabling full participation for this group of learners in the school and wider community.

The word *independence* also routinely features in key definitions of wellbeing, particularly, as we will see in Chapter 4, in public policy. In the next chapter, we explore to what extent recent research and literature help us understand the concept of independence with respect to young people with PMLD.

Reference list

Bellamy, G., Croot, L., Bush, A., Berry, H., & Smith, A. (2010). A study to define profound and multiple learning disabilities (PMLD). *Journal of Intellectual Disabilities*, *14*(3), 221–235.

Better Outcomes New Delivery (BOND). (2013). *Children and young people with learning disabilities – Understanding their mental health*. London: Young Minds.

Bouras, N., Hardy, S., & Holt, G. (2011). *Mental health in intellectual disabilities: A reader* (4th ed.). Brighton: Pavilion.

Bradley, E., Summers, J., Wood, H. L., & Bryson, S. (2004). Comparing rates of psychiatric and behavior disorders in adolescents and young adults with severe intellectual disability with and without autism. *Journal of Autism and Developmental Disorders*, *34*(2), 151–161.

Carpenter, B., Egerton, J., Cockbill, B., Bloom, T., Fotheringham, J., Rawson, H., & Thistlethwaite, J. (2015). *Engaging learners with complex learning difficulties and disabilities*. London: Routledge.

Dee, L., Byers, R., Hayhoe, H., & Maudslay, L. (2002). *Enhancing quality of life: Facilitating transitions for people with profound and complex learning difficulties*. Cambridge: National Bureau for Students with Disabilities.

De Haas, C. (2020). Singing together: Friends' and families' perspectives on ways to be included in society. In M. Nind & I. Strnadova (Eds.), *Belonging for people with profound intellectual and multiple disabilities* (pp. 159–175). London: Routledge.

Fox, M., Laverty, T., & Chowdhury, S. (2020). *Supporting the emotional wellbeing of children and young people with learning disabilities*. London: Routledge.

Frogley, G., & Welch, J. (1993). *A pictorial history of Netherne hospital*. Redhill: East Surrey Area Health Authority.

Glover, G., & Ayub, M. (2010). *How people with learning disabilities die. Improving health and lives*. Durham: Learning Disabilities Observatory.

Grant, G., Goward, P., Richardson, M., & Ramcharan, P. (2010). *Learning disability: A life cycle approach to valuing people* (2nd ed.). Maidenhead: Open University Press.

Hanisch, H. (2014). Recognising disability. In J. Bickenbach, F. Felder, & B. Schmitz (Eds.), *Disability and the good human life* (pp. 113–138). Cambridge: Cambridge University Press.

Hoskin, J. (Ed.). (2018). *A guide to duchene muscular dystrophy*. London: Jessica Kingsley Publishers.

Imray, P., & Colley, A. (2017). *Inclusion is dead. Long live inclusion*. London: Routledge.

Johnson, K., & Walmsley, J. (2010.). *People with intellectual disabilities. Towards a good life?* Bristol: The Policy Press.

Kamstra, A., van der Putten, A., & Vlaskamp, C. (2015). The structure of intellectual and multiple disabilities. *Journal of Applied Research in Intellectual Disabilities, 28*, 249–256.

Lacey, P., & Scull, J. (2015). Inclusive education for learners with severe, profound and multiple learning difficulties in England. *Including Learners with Low-Incidence Disabilities, 5*, 241–268.

Lyons, G., & Cassebohm, M. (2012). Student wellbeing for those with profound intellectual and multiple disabilities: Same, or same but different? *Journal of Student Wellbeing, 5*(2), 18–33.

Maes, B., Penne, A., Vastmans, K., & Arthur-Kelley, M. (2020). Inclusion and participation of students with profound intellectual and multiple difficulties. In M. Nind & I. Strnadova (Eds.), *Belonging for people with profound intellectual and multiple disabilities* (pp. 41–58). London: Routledge.

Matson, J., Gardner, W., Coe, D., & Sovner, R. (1991). A scale for evaluating emotional disorders in severely and profoundly mentally retarded persons. Development of the diagnostic assessment for the severely handicapped (DASH) scale. *The British Journal of Psychiatry: The Journal of Mental Science, 159*, 404–409.

National Association of Independent and Non-Maintained Special Schools (NASS). (2017). Retrieved from www.nasschools.org.uk/

NHS. (2020). *Angleman syndrome*. Retrieved from www.nhs.uk/conditions/angelman-syndrome/

Nijs, S. (2020, May). Peer Interactions among persons with profound intellectual and multiple disabilities. In D. Toubert-Duffort & E. Atlan (Eds.), *La Nouvelle Revue: Education et société inclusive. Polyhandicap et processus d'apprentissage* (Vol. 88, pp. 153–169). Paris: INSHEA.

Nijs, S., Vlaskamp, C., & Maes, B. (2016). Children with PIMD in interaction with peers with PIMD or siblings. *Journal of Intellectual Disability Research, 60*(1), 28–42.

Nind, M., & Strnadova, I. (2020). Changes in the lives of people with PIMD. In M. Nind & I. Strnadova (Eds.), *Belonging for people with profound intellectual and multiple disabilities* (pp. 1–21). London: Routledge.

Nussbaum, M. C. (2007). *Frontiers of justice – Disability, nationality, species membership.* Cambridge, MA: Harvard University Press.

O'Brien, J. (2016). *Don't send him in tomorrow. Shining a light on the marginalized, disenfranchised and forgotten children of today's schools.* Carmarthen: Independent Thinking Press.

Prudhomme, D., Geiger, M., Luger, R., & Bullen, A. (2018). Simple ideas that work: Celebrating development in persons with profound intellectual and multiple disabilities. *African Journal of Disability, 7*(1), 1–10.

Rose, R., Hawley, M., Fergusson, A., & Jament, J. (2009). Mental health and special educational needs: Exploring a complex relationship. *British Journal of Special Education, 36*(1), 3–8.

Schuller, T., & Watson, D. (2009). *Learning through life.* Leicester: NIACE.

Sen, A. (1999). *Commodities and capabilities (Oxford India paperbacks).* Oxford: Oxford University Press.

Shakespeare, T. (2014). *Disability rights and wrongs* (2nd ed.). London: Routledge.

Simmons, B., & Watson, B. (2014). *The PMLD ambiguity.* London: Karnak Books Limited.

Taylor, B. (2014). *The last asylum – A memoir of madness in our times.* London: Penguin.

Ware, J. (2017, September). *Assessment for learners with PMLD.* Paper presented at BERA Annual Conference, Brighton.

Weare, K. (2015). *What works in promoting social and emotional wellbeing and responding to mental health problems in schools? Advice for schools and framework document.* London: National Children's Bureau.

3 What do we mean by independence?

What is independence?

In the same way that, in the last chapter, we looked at how writers and researchers have tried to define *wellbeing* with respect to young people with PMLD, in this chapter, we do the same with a term which has a great deal of currency not only in special education but in all areas of education as well: *independence*.

Independence, according to Jordan (2013), is a "mark of adult status" (p. 209), and for Kittay (2011), it is a norm of human functioning, and yet one of the agreed-on criteria within any of the most commonly used – and almost universally agreed – definitions of profound and multiple learning difficulties (PMLD) is that people with PMLD will be dependent on the support of others for their whole lives. This then immediately puts them at odds with what Goodley, Runswick Cole and Lidiard (2016) call "the normative stuff of everyday human life" (p. 772) and which Johnson and Walmsley (2010) describe as the "individualism which reflects the current values of the wider society – a home, a paid job, choice and control" (p. 112). Aird (2001) sees this essential exclusion of young people with PMLD from the independence agenda as a growing problem, lamenting that "the increasing influence of the enterprise culture does not and cannot work in favour of pupils with PMLD" (p. 29). The imperative to be independent in everyday life (Taylor, 2014) is stronger than ever, and needing other people on a day-to-day basis is seen as "a mark of emotional debility" (ibid, p. 248). Those therefore for whom conventional notions of independence are

DOI: 10.4324/9781003097648-4

elusive effectively remain in a kind of childlike state of dependency, trapped at the very far end of what Nussbaum (2007) calls the "single linear ranking of relative social positions" (p. 141) exacerbated by the "cultural assumption that disability is associated with dependency, invalidity and tragedy" (Shakespeare, 2014 p. 17).

As with *wellbeing* and *community participation*, there may then need to be a redefinition of *independence* for people with PMLD, and in fact, there have been attempts in the literature to put forward definitions of independence which can take account of the unique needs and profiles of those with PMLD. Vorhaus (2015) for example defines independence in terms of its "related freedoms – especially freedom of movement, action and choice" (p. 32), Kittay (2011) feels that independence for people with more complex needs involves "the capacity to choose, act for oneself and develop one's potential" (p. 49), and Nussbaum (2007) refines the notion of 'choice' with respect to people with disabilities as control over one's environment, a point we will see echoed around the world in many of the responses to the *Lives Lived Well* surveys in Part II. Johnson and Walmsley (2010) believe that a good life for people with complex needs can be an independent life, whereby someone has the means to choose what to do, when to do it and who to do it with, and Dee, Byers, Hayhoe and Maudslay (2002) suggest that independence is characterised simply by choices and lifestyle decisions regardless of the support that is required to realise those options in practical terms.

Choice?

We are hearing and will hear in Part II of this book, a lot of this word *choice*, but 'choice' perhaps, as we normally understand it, can become problematic where opportunities for the young person's voice to be heard are limited by aspects of their condition (McKay, 2014). Woolf (2010) reminds us starkly that without a voice or conventional pathways for expressing choice, the lives of people with PMLD run the risk of becoming nothing more than an "epiphenomenon – or by-product – of other people's decisions" (p. 153), and this is echoed by De Haas (2020), who cites Swinton, Mowat and Baines (2011) that people with PMLD may become victims of constructions of their stories that they do not own. In other words, the 'choices' they appear to make are, in fact,

Voice?

But moving on from Christmas cards, choice and involvement in decision-making for a person with PMLD very often does, of course, rely on the advocacy or interpretation of others, usually their parents and carers. Maes, Penne, Vastmans and Arthur-Kelley (2020) call this 'knowingness' or in other words the ability of people around the child to tune into their shared meanings and lived experience. There can be no doubt, of course, that the people who know them best do provide a window on the young person's social world (De Haas, 2020), and as we will see in Part II, many different voices around the child can enable that child to speak. But this can in itself be a restricting factor to achieving any form of independence (Simmons & Watson, 2014). Professor Robin Banerjee of the University of Sussex speaking at the July 2019 SEN Policy Research Forum in London commented perhaps controversially that sometimes parents are the wrong people to ask, echoing Dee et al.'s (2002) concern that it can be "almost impossible to distinguish between the views and needs of the child and those of their parents" (p. 8). Pellicano et al. (2014) identified these issues when working with the parents of children with complex needs. Some parents, they found, explained how their child "doesn't speak" and so "couldn't make a decision" (p. 44). Another mother remarked how her child "hasn't got a clue at all. So those decisions just have to be made for him" (p. 44). Even in school settings (Johnson & Walmsley, 2010), the staff around the person can reduce their independence further if they are "cast as a way to compensate for a perceived lack of reason" (p. 151), but we are back with the Christmas cards again and reiterating that even the best and most highly trained staff members, and with the best will in the world, can make assumptions about what the young person might have chosen to do or say if they had a 'voice' or, in an even more extreme example, assumptions about what that young person would do or say if they did not have special needs. We must never forget, of course, that the parents' experience of bringing up a child with PMLD can often have been a difficult and often traumatic one (Toubert-Duffort & Atlan, 2020) and that, for that very reason, parents do very often need to share their voices with someone who has a more objective view of the child, but at the same time, parents can also often feel excluded from discussions amongst professionals concerning their child. In these cases, it is up to the professionals to mediate and interpret the understandably emotional responses of the parents.

Returning to the voice of the child him or herself, I think we can all agree that there can be a tendency to underestimate the complexity of the thinking and intentions that children with PMLD are capable of (Brigg, Schuitema, & Vorhaus, 2017), although Nind and Strnadova (2020) acknowledge that – albeit slowly – the capacity of people with PMLD is being more widely appreciated. It is important then to find innovative ways of listening and understanding (Nussbaum, 2007; Whitehurst, 2007) with a full appreciation of the combination of verbal, gestural, bodily and other means of conveying meaning (Maes et al., 2020) which a person with PMLD is capable of. Nijs (2020) calls these "idiosyncratic signals" (p. 154), and understanding these signals is achieved through meticulous planning (Palikara, Castro, Gaona, & Vasiliki, 2018) and by using a "plurality of methods" (Danieli & Woodhams, 2005, p. 285) with an emphasis (Jones & Riley, 2017) on a nuanced appreciation of a pupil's communication which recognises not just words but incidental cues and engagement. We will find out in Part II some of the many innovative ways schools around the world seek to understand the communication of their learners with PMLD.

Dependent but also independent?

How else then might *independence* be redefined for this group of people? And let's not forget that there are more than 11,000 young people with PMLD in schools and possibly as many 75,000 of all ages in the UK, and they all deserve to feel at least as independent as the rest of us. Kittay (2011) reminds us that we all "selves-in-relation" (p. 54), in other words, that we exist very largely with and around others, and the fact that each human being (Vorhaus, 2015) is extensively dependent on other people is an "obvious basic truth that does not always get the attention it deserves" (p. 55). Dependence, according to Vorhaus, "is not equivalent to helplessness or passivity" (p 43). We all have long and short periods of dependency (Kittay, 2011), and true independence is rooted in social connection. In reality, "people depend on other people to lead a liveable life" (ibid, p. 264), and the quality and shape of social networks are central to the wellbeing of us all. This truth was, of course, again brought home to all of us during the COVID-19 pandemic when the number of people we could depend on – socially, emotionally, physically – became drastically reduced and, not surprisingly, rates of anxiety and depression went up.

Here again, the Capabilities Approach (Nussbaum, 2007) helps us see dependency and the need for care as "inseparable features of the human condition and consequently of social order as well" (Vehmas, 2014, p. 307). Dignity, something we all so desperately want to preserve for these young people, can also be found "in relations of dependency" (Nussbaum, 2007, p. 218), because only then will we be able to create what Nussbaum calls "a full and equal citizenship of people with physical impairments, and of those who care for them" (p. 99). Dependency, for Kittay (2011), is support with understanding and is "often compatible with fulfilling and reciprocal relationships" (Kittay, 2011, p. 52). Assistance, Kittay argues, should not be seen as a limitation, or something 'less than', but as an indispensable resource at the basis of a vision of society that is able to take full account of relationships of dependency, ensuring a fulfilling life both for the carer and the cared for.

Nussbaum, in fact, sees her 10 key Human Capabilities as being applicable equally to the person with disabilities as well as to their parents or guardians. Issues of independence and wellbeing are just as important for the carer as for the cared for, but sadly both are "stigmatised by dependency" (Kittay, p. 51). Parents and carers (Simmons & Watson, 2014) will have no choice but to be closely linked to those with PMLD for the rest of their lives, and to explore this further, the *Lives Lived Well* survey asked how schools involve parents and carers in the school life of their child. We will hear what they say in Part II.

Personal and sexual independence?

Finally, it is important to remember here that "managing self-care" (Jordan, 2013, p. 223) is a mark of independence for all young people but one which, as we have seen and will look at again later, needs to be sensitively supported by understanding carers so that the young person does not feel they are being disempowered in the process. One aspect of this is the right of young people with PMLD just like anyone else to "develop and express themselves as sexual beings" (ibid, p. 232). Sexualised behaviour by young learners with PMLD can present the greatest challenge for parents, carers and teachers (Longhorn, 1997), and Liddiard and Slater (2017) and Goodley et al. (2016) show that whilst measures to suppress the sexual choices and expressions in young people with PMLD may not now be as drastic as they once were (Tarnai, 2006), this group does nevertheless lack sexual autonomy. To a certain extent, this may be understandable in the light of the "potential constraints of having a body which is looked after by others" (p. 17), but nevertheless, there is a real concern that sex education and support are denied to this group and that "the sexual selves of disabled people are routinely problematised, and, in some contexts, deemed uncontrollable and in need of containment" (Goodley et al., 2016, p. 779). We asked the participants in the UK survey how they think a young person with PMLD can be supported to express themselves as sexual beings, and as we will see in Part II, the question produced some of the most interesting results in the whole survey.

So we have looked quite closely, I hope, in these last two chapters at how wellbeing and independence have been defined by writers and researchers in the field of special education. In the next chapter, we will see what policy, both in the UK and internationally, has to say about these two terms with respect to people with PMLD.

Reference list

Aird, R. (2001). *The education and care of children with severe, profound and multiple learning difficulties.* London: David Fulton Publishers.

Banerjee., R. (2019, July). *Personal, social, and emotional learning: Accountability and outcomes.* Paper presented at Accountability, performance management and inspection: How to enable positive responses to diversity? Special Educational Needs Policy Research Forum, London.

Brigg, G., Schuitema, K., & Vorhaus, J. (2017). Children with profound and multiple learning difficulties: Laughter, capability and relating to others. *Disability & Society*, *31*(9), 1175–1189.

Danieli, A., & Woodhams, C. (2005). Emancipatory research methodology and disability. *International Journal of Social Research Methodology*, *8*(4), 281–296.

Dee, L., Byers, R., Hayhoe, H., & Maudslay, L. (2002). *Enhancing quality of life: Facilitating transitions for people with profound and complex learning difficulties*. Cambridge: National Bureau for Students with Disabilities.

De Haas, C. (2020). Singing together: Friends' and families' perspectives on ways to be included in society. In M. Nind & I. Strnadova (Eds.), *Belonging for people with profound intellectual and multiple disabilities* (pp. 159–175). London: Routledge.

Goodley, D., Runswick Cole, K., & Lidiard, K. (2016). The Dishman child discourse. *Studies in the Cultural Politics of Education*, *37*(5), 770–784.

Johnson, K., & Walmsley, J. (2010). *People with intellectual disabilities. Towards a good life?* Bristol: The Policy Press.

Jones, P., & Riley, M. (2017). Trying, failing, succeeding, and trying again and again: Perspectives of teachers of pupils with severe profound multiple learning difficulties. *European Journal of Teacher Education*, *40*(2), 271–285.

Jordan, R. (2013). *Autism with severe learning difficulties* (2nd ed.). London: Souvenir Press.

Kittay, E. (2011). The ethics of care, dependence and disability. *Ratio Juris*, *24*(1), 49–58.

Liddiard, K., & Slater, J. (2017). Like, pissing yourself is not a particularly attractive quality, let's be honest: Learning to contain through youth, adulthood, disability and sexuality. *Sexualities*, 1461–7382. doi. org/10.1177/1363460716688674

Longhorn, F. (1997). *Sex education and sexuality for very special people – A sensory approach*. Bedford: Catalyst Education Resources Limited.

Maes, B., Penne, A., Vastmans, K., & Arthur-Kelley, M. (2020). Inclusion and participation of students with profound intellectual and multiple difficulties. In M. Nind & I. Strnadova (Eds.), *Belonging for people with profound intellectual and multiple disabilities* (pp. 41–58). London: Routledge.

McKay, J. (2014). Young people's voices: Disciplining young people's participation in decision making in special educational needs. *Journal of Education Policy*, *29*(6), 760–773.

Nijs, S. (2020, May). Peer Interactions among persons with profound intellectual and multiple disabilities. In D. Toubert-Duffort & E. Atlan (Eds.), *La Nouvelle Revue: Education et société inclusive. Polyhandicap et processus d'apprentissage* (Vol. 88, pp. 153–169). Paris: INSHEA.

Nind, M., & Strnadova, I. (2020). Changes in the lives of people with PIMD. In M. Nind & I. Strnadova (Eds.), *Belonging for people with profound intellectual and multiple disabilities* (pp. 1–21). London: Routledge.

Nussbaum, M. C. (2007). *Frontiers of justice – Disability, nationality, species membership.* Cambridge, MA: Harvard University Press.

Palikara, O., Castro, S., Gaona, C., & Vasiliki, E. (2018). Capturing the voices of children in the EHC plans: Are we there yet? *Frontiers in Education, 3*(24). doi:10.3389/feduc.2018.00024

Pellicano, L., Hill, V., Croydon, A., Greathead, S., Kenny, L., & Yates, R. (2014). *My life at school: Understanding the experiences of children and young people with special educational needs in residential special schools.* London: Office of the Children's Commissioner.

Shakespeare, T. (2014). *Disability rights and wrongs* (2nd ed.). London: Routledge.

Simmons, B., & Watson, B. (2014). *The PMLD ambiguity.* London: Karnak Books Limited.

Swinton, J., Mowat, H., & Baines, S. (2011). Whose story am I? Redescribing profound intellectual disability in the kingdom of God. *Journal of Religion, Disability and Health, 15*(1), 5–19.

Tarnai, B. (2006). Review of effective interventions for socially inappropriate masturbation in persons with cognitive disabilities. *Sexuality and Disability, 24*(3), 151–168.

Taylor, B. (2014). *The last asylum – A memoir of madness in our times.* London: Penguin.

Toubert-Duffort, D., & Atlan, E. (Eds.). (2020, May). *La Nouvelle Revue: Education et société inclusive. Polyhandicap et processus d'apprentissage* (Vol. 88, pp. 153–169). Paris: INSHEA.

Vehmas, S. (2014). What can philosophy tell us about disability? In N. Watson, A. Roulstone, & C. Thomas (Eds.), *The Routledge handbook of disability studies* (pp. 298–309). London: Routledge.

Vorhaus, J. (2015). *Giving voice to profound disability.* London: Routledge.

Whitehurst, T. (2007). Liberating silent voices – Perspectives of children with profound and complex learning needs on inclusion. *British Journal of Learning Disabilities, 35*, 55–61.

Woolf, J. (2010). Cognitive disability in a society of equals. In E. Kittay & L. Carlson (Eds.), *Cognitive disability and its challenge for moral philosophy* (pp. 147–159). Chichester: Wiley-Blackwell.

Wellbeing and independence in international and UK national policy

We have talked in Chapters 2 and 3 about what writers and researchers have said about the meanings of 'wellbeing' and 'independence', so now to finish Part I, we ask how these sometimes hotly debated terms are defined in international and UK policy.

International policy

The Organisation for Economic Co-operation and Development acknowledges that "there is no single definition of wellbeing" (2011, p. 18), so definitions "may vary by context and shift over time" (Anand, 2016, p. 4), although the World Health Organisation (WHO; 2018) does describe "a state of wellbeing in which every individual recognises his or her own potential, can cope with the normal stresses of life, can work productively and fruitfully, and is able to make contributions to his or her community" (para. 1). Inherent in these definitions are issues of independence, although, as seen in the WHO definition, close links between independence, employment and community participation can make these definitions difficult to apply to people with profound and multiple learning disabilities (PMLD).

There is also a clear commitment in international policy to the wellbeing of young people in particular. In 2008 for instance, the United Nations General Assembly reaffirmed the commitment it made to the

United Nations Children's Fund's 2002 paper 'A World Fit for Children' (pp. 67–68):

- To respect the dignity and to secure the wellbeing of all children

- To promote healthy lives

- To listen to children and ensure their participation.

A World Fit for Children was itself a reaffirmation of Article 12 of the UN Convention on the Rights of the Child (1989) which asserted the rights of children to be included in decision making around issues which affect them, and the UN-commissioned Stiglitz Report (2009) called for countries to shift emphasis away from measuring economic production to measuring people's wellbeing.

With respect to people with disabilities in particular, article 3 (a) of the UN Convention on the Rights of Persons with Disabilities (2007) affirms the general principals of

- respect for inherent dignity,

- individual autonomy,

- the freedom to make one's own choices and

- independence of persons.

UK government policy

In the UK policy context, Bickenbach (2014) has shown that this international commitment to wellbeing has been echoed in initiatives such as the 'Wellbeing Manifesto for a Flourishing Society' (Shah & Marks, 2014) which was drawn up in association with the New Economics Foundation and in the 2010 Coalition government commitments to measure quality of life. More recently, Public Health England produced guidance around wellbeing as part of the wider 'All Our Health Guide', which is described as "a resource for all health and care professionals to help you use your knowledge, skills and relationships to prevent ill-

30 Part I

ness, protect health and promote wellbeing" (Public Health England, 2019).

Whilst on the subject of policy in England, it is worth returning briefly to the issue of sexual autonomy discussed towards the end of the last chapter. In a *Guardian* newspaper article in June 2020, Amelia Hill reported that the court of appeal in England had overturned an earlier ruling that a man has a "fundamental right to sex", even though he cannot understand the issue of consent. The overturning of this ruling clearly has implications for the future sexual autonomy of people with PMLD and will need to be followed closely by all those who work with or care for these young people.

Educational policy in England

Turning now to educational policy in England, the following key documents, all from the Department of Health (DoH) underpinned and informed the most recent policy and in particular the *Special Educational Needs and Disability Code of Practice* (2015) which is a statutory document for English schools under the Part 3 of the Children and Families Act (2014) and which we discuss in more detail later:

> *Valuing People* (DoH, 2001) Government White Paper: 'A new strategy for learning disability for the 21st century based on social inclusion, civil rights, choice and independence'. (p. 14)
> *Aiming High for Disabled Children* (DoH, 2007) Policy Document: 'The vision behind Aiming High for Disabled Children is for all families with disabled children to have the support they need to live ordinary family lives, as a matter of course'. (p. 4)
> *Valuing People Now* (DoH, 2009) Policy Document: 'what needs to be done to make the lives of people with learning disabilities better'. (p. 4)

Valuing People Now (DoH, 2009) restated the commitment made in *Valuing People* (DoH, 2001) that all people with learning difficulties should have "the same opportunities as other people in society to lead a fulfilling life" (p. 3). It is reasonable to assume that this includes those with PMLD, as *Valuing People, Aiming High for Disabled Children* and

Valuing People Now all use forms of the term 'profound and multiple learning difficulties', although at different frequencies. *Valuing People* has 18 instances of the term 'profound disabilities' and affirms that everyone should be able to make choices and that "this includes people with severe and profound disabilities" (p. 24). *Aiming High for Disabled Children* mentions 'profound disabilities' once and 'complex needs' 8 times in its 61 pages, and *Valuing People Now* has 7 mentions of 'profound disabilities' and 45 of 'complex needs' in its 146 pages. However, Nind and Strnadova (2020) find that this group did not benefit sufficiently from policy changes such as *Valuing People* and are poorly supported in the transition to adulthood, although *Valuing People Now* did to a certain extent acknowledge that.

Although *wellbeing* as a term is not common in any of these three documents, its relative prevalence does reflect its growing importance in education policy and debate in the 21st century. In 2001, *Valuing People* only used the term once; in 2007, *Aiming High for Disabled Children*, five times; and by 2009, *Valuing People Now*, the number of instances had risen to nine.

All three policy documents make it clear that independence is a key aim for people with all disabilities, though without ever discussing in any depth what independence means for those with PMLD: *Valuing People* is very clear in its aims to "provide new opportunities for children and adults with learning disabilities and their families to live full and independent lives as part of their local communities" (p. 2), *Aiming High for Disabled Children* emphasises that support at the transition to adulthood is vital to enable disabled young people to gain independence, and *Valuing People Now* is clear that "the starting presumption should be one of independence, rather than dependence" (p. 23), so as identified in some of literature we discussed in Chapters 2 and 3, an approach to 'independence' which does not seem to take account of the actual lives of people with PMLD.

Echoing Johnson and Walmsley's (2010) question, "How do we find out what people with disabilities want?" (p. 49), the documents address some of the complex issues around communication for young people with PMLD which we discuss in other parts of this book. *Valuing People*, for instance, asserts that "people with profound and complex disabilities may have difficulty communicating their needs and wishes. They may need the support of someone who knows them well such as

32 Part I

a family member, an advocate or a supporter" (p. 101). *Valuing People Now* discusses the development and use of appropriate communication systems for people who have little or no verbal communication, taking guidance "from families and friends to understand what gestures or sounds may mean" (p. 38).

Possibly reflecting its greater focus on young people with PMLD, *Valuing People Now* devotes a page to Intensive Interaction (Hewett, 2018) as an aid to communication, although generally, these documents frame communication in terms of "communication techniques and new technology" (*Valuing People*, 2001, p. 32), "assistance with communication" (ibid, p. 94), "communication systems" (*Valuing People Now*, DoH, 2009 p. 40) and "aids to communication" (pp. 75, 111), implying that what is required is simply something to replace conventional speech. Ouvry (1987) and Jordan (2013) have found, however, that a taught alternative to conventional speech, such as a sign- or a symbol-based system, may not be the answer to most communication difficulties in young people with PMLD in which the social context and the cultural transmissions (Jordan, 2013) which accompany conventional speech have not followed what we might call predictable or neurotypical patterns.

Employment is routinely cited as an indicator of wellbeing and independence in these documents despite the fact that (Shakespeare, 2014) a very significant proportion of all people with learning difficulties have little prospect of performing basic work skills in what has become known as a 'knowledge economy' or, in other words, an economy which prizes high skill levels over all else. *Aiming High for Disabled Children* states that "employment is a major aspiration for people with learning disabilities," (p. 18), and *Valuing People Now* talks about the "presumption of employability" (p. 88) and that "the vision for people with more complex needs is the same as for everyone: inclusion and participation in all areas of community life, including living independently and having paid work" (p. 34). *Valuing People Now* is even more precise that people with learning difficulties "have a role to play as contributors . . . and should be supported to work, pay taxes, vote, do jury duty, have children" (p. 33). The assumption seems to be then that "with the right help and support" (*Valuing People*, DoH, 2001, p. 24), all people with learning difficulties, including presumably those with PMLD, can achieve the same forms of wellbeing and independence as everyone else.

The inclusion of voting in one of these indicators of independence is worth discussing a bit further. It is unlikely that someone with PMLD as defined in any of the ways described in the introduction to this book will be able to understand the voting process, and in some cases, their ability to navigate a polling station independently or the impact of their behaviours may make it unlikely that they will be able to vote in person. The alternative is to appoint a proxy to vote on their behalf as outlined by the Electoral Commission (2019) in its document *Application to vote by proxy based on disability*, which tells the voter who isn't able to cast their vote in person:

> you can have someone you trust cast your vote for you . . . You must ask someone who is willing and capable to be your proxy and vote on your behalf . . . You must give a reason why you need to vote by proxy and may need a qualified person to sign your application.
>
> (p. 1)

A condition of being allowed a proxy vote is that the primary voter must "let your proxy know how you want them to vote on your behalf, for example, which candidate, party, or outcome" (p. 2), and the primary voter must be able to provide a response to the following: "I am not able to go to the polling station on election day due to the following disability" (p. 3).

These criteria effectively disenfranchise tens of thousands of people of voting age in the UK who also happen to have PMLD. Nussbaum (2007) suggests a solution but one which again would require a rethinking of meanings of *independence* and *dependence*. She suggests that a parent or other guardian voting on behalf of someone with PMLD is, in fact, enfranchising that person even where they are incapable of "forming a view and communicating that view to a guardian" (Nussbaum, 2010, p. 88). What is more, Nussbaum concludes, if we allow a parent or guardian to vote on behalf of the person with PMLD, "the very presence of the surrogate serves to give due recognition to the person with a disability and to persons with disability more generally" (p. 93).

We can see then that key international policy documents as well as recent UK national educational policy around special needs have not taken full account of the needs and profiles of those with PMLD, often because judgements about their lives and achievements are based on the experiences and values of the policy makers (Nussbaum, 2007) or because all types and levels of disability are seen as effectively the same and, finally, because people with PMLD tend to be viewed as non-contributors to a society built around production for profit.

So let's now turn to the policy document whose 290 or so pages everyone in the UK who works with or is in any way involved with anyone with learning difficulties has had to grapple with since 2014: the *Special Educational Needs and Disabilities Code of Practice* (DfE, 2015). This has been described as the most substantial change in special education policy in the last two decades (Palikara, Castro, Gaona, & Vasiliki, 2018) and the most significant for 30 years (Hoskin, 2018), so we need to examine how it defines and discusses wellbeing and independence with respect to learners with PMLD.

The Special Educational Needs and Disabilities (SEND) Code of Practice (2015)

The *SEND Code of Practice* (SENCoP, 2015) is statutory guidance. It is outcome-based, and outcomes are "the basis on which provision is made and resources allocated" (Catlin, 2018, p. 150). Outcomes must focus on what "matters to the young person" (SENCoP, 2015, p. 137) and should include positive outcomes within wider areas of "personal and social development" (p. 25) and "levels of mental health and wellbeing' (p. 46). These outcomes should be "SMART (specific, measurable, achievable, realistic, time-bound)" (p. 160), although many practitioners working with young people with PMLD (Imray & Colley, 2017) have questioned whether linear or SMART outcomes are appropriate for this group, and we will see in Part II that these sentiments are very much echoed in responses to the *Lives Lived Well* surveys.

'Wellbeing', which is often used in the document alongside the words *health* and *mental health*, is a key issue then in current SEND policy, and there are 21 occurrences of the term *wellbeing* in the *SEND Code of Practice* (2015). Local authorities must "promote . . . children and young people's wellbeing" (p. 24), and in fact, the words *promote* and *improve* are frequently used alongside the term *wellbeing* in the document. There is also a clear expectation that local authorities must "explicitly have regard to the wellbeing of parent carers" (p. 72) and an acknowledgement that "loss of paid employment can have a significant impact on the carer's wellbeing" (p. 19).

There is also an emphasis within the *SEND Code of Practice* (2015), on "community participation" as an indicator of wellbeing (p. 124), with a specific acknowledgement of the importance for young people with more complex needs "to participate actively in their local community" (p. 47). Outcomes for learners with all levels of need should include those within wider areas of "personal and social development" (p. 25), as well as "positive social relationships" (p. 163), and there is a clear expectation that local authorities, education providers and their partners should work together to help children and young people to realise their ambitions in relation to "participating in society – including having friends and supportive relationships, and participating in, and contributing to, the local community" (p. 28).

Independence in the *SEND Code of Practice* (2015) is also seen as a prerequisite to achieving "self-esteem" (p. 123) echoing concerns expressed earlier in the chapter that any forms of dependency are considered to be inherently undesirable. The document aims to "promote independence and self-advocacy" (p. 32), help children gain independence and "prepare for adult life" (p. 120), "promote greater independence and learn important life skills" (p. 124) and "achieve independence in all aspects of life" (p. 295). There are also, however, the same discrepancies we discussed earlier under 'policy' when discussing 'independence', discrepancies between conventional definitions of independence and the actual lives of people with PMLD, with independence itself commonly linked to 'independent living' and 'employment'. Chapter 8 of the *SEND Code of Practice*, 'Preparing for Adulthood From the Earliest Years', is very explicit that adulthood means preparing for

- higher education and/or employment – this includes exploring different employment options, such as support for becoming self-employed and help from supported employment agencies. (p. 28)

Here again, the needs and profiles of those with PMLD as defined in the introduction to this book are not accounted for. Burch (2017) undertakes a fascinating critical discourse analysis of the *SEND Code of Practice* (2015) in which she deconstructs notions of independence as they are

36 Part I

expressed in the document and suggests that the document has been "written in accordance with the economic concerns of the country, rather than the individual needs of children and young people" (p. 2). She identifies the fact that "the notion of adulthood in the Code is a recurring topic" (p. 2) and that a "commitment to independent living as well as support for students with SEN [special educational needs] is placed firmly in the realm of employability" (p. 2), with employability seen as an "outcome of education" for everybody (p. 7). Independence, she notes, is justified on the grounds of "economic utility" (p. 9) and is firmly based on labour-market criteria.

As we have already seen, a common indicator of independence is the ability to communicate clear choices and opinions. Section 19 of the Children and Families Act 2014, of which the *SEND Code of Practice* is a pivotal part, makes clear also that when supporting young people with special needs, local authorities must have regard for the views of the young person, and the *SEND Code of Practice* itself affirms this in asserting that young people should be able to "participate fully in decisions about the outcomes they wish to achieve" (p. 33), although communication within the document is framed in terms of conventional speech or a close substitute and "the development of good language" (p. 47), so not the less typical but equally valid means of communication we see in young people with PMLD.

Decisions by a young person recorded in their Education, Health and Care (EHC) Plan will typically "involve discussion with their family and others, but the final decision rests with the young person" (p. 127). Here again, however, Palikara et al. (2018) note that there is limited systematic evidence to date on how the voices of children who do not communicate conventionally are recorded in their EHC Plans, which nevertheless *must* include the child's own voice, and often, there is no indication in the plans on how the child's views are interpreted by the parent or other representing adults.

It is, of course, important to remember that one of the innovations of the *SEND Code of Practice* was the provision of services from birth to 25 years and therefore should underpin the young person's transition from school to a college or other post-19 provision. Nind and Strnadova (2020) have real concerns in this area which we will see echoed in many of the responses to the *Lives Lived Well* surveys. They acknowledge that the journey through the education system involves many different challenges for people with PMLD but that the cracks that open at the transition from school are so severe that there is a danger that not just their skills and prior learning but also parts of their history will be left behind as they move on. Exacerbating this further (Gauthier-Boudreault, Beaudoin, Gallagher, & Couture, 2017), there is also the simple fact that there is a scarcity of post-school services for people with PMLD.

Before concluding this section on statutory policy, it is important not to overlook official policy in the UK around school effectiveness, and we will visit this topic again when we look at the work of Chailey Heritage School in Part III. In January 2019, the Office for Standards in Education (Ofsted) published its new Education Inspection Framework (EIF). Covering all schools – including special schools – there is an acknowledgement within the EIF that providers should "support learners to develop their character – including their resilience, confidence and independence – and help them know how to keep physically and mentally healthy" (p. 11). However, as with other policy documents discussed earlier, the concept of 'independence' continues to be linked with "employment or training" (p. 10).

There is a concern then that key UK educational policy documents of the 21st century do not adequately account for young people with PMLD and do not allow for holistic outcomes such as social and domestic outcomes, wellbeing and outcomes for parents and carers, and as we will see in the next part, teachers and other practitioners expressed very strong opinions about this in the *Lives Lived Well* survey. Schools in the UK at least, can, however, also access non-statutory guidance which is, in some cases, endorsed by the UK government, and we now briefly look at two of these in the next sections and ask whether they address more effectively the unique needs of young people with PMLD.

The PMLD Essential Service Standards

The PMLD Essential Service Standards (Doukas, Fergusson, Fullerton, & Grace, 2017) are endorsed by the UK government as well as NHS England. They are designed to create a means for commissioners of education, health and social care to work closely in partnership with

38 Part I

service providers such as schools to ensure the best possible outcomes for people with PMLD.

There are standards for organisations as well as for individuals around wellbeing, communication and social, community and family and the approach to these key concepts addresses some of the concerns outlined earlier by accounting specifically for the needs of young people with PMLD and their families. With respect to wellbeing for instance, there is a "clear focus on postural care management and a recognition of the holistic vulnerability of people with profound and multiple learning disabilities" (p. 30). Community participation, according to the standards, is about supporting "each person to maintain strong family and friend contacts" and creating "new opportunities for people and their families to form wider social relationships" (p. 26). Social and community life for young people with PMLD should be about "thriving and not just surviving" (p. 33) and being "visible and actively involved in their communities" (p. 33). Independence is about being "empowered and enabled to do things" (p. 32), and organisations are encouraged to provide "carefully risk assessed and planned opportunities to enhance independence" (p. 26). There is also a focus on "communication in its entirety" (p. 28) and an acknowledgement that communication should be a collaborative activity supported by trained and properly resourced people who "develop warm and trusting relationships" (p. 24) with the young person.

Preparing for Adulthood

The Preparing for Adulthood (PfA, 2020; www.preparingforadulthood. org.uk,) programme is funded by the Department for Education (DfE) as part of the Delivering Better Outcomes Together consortium. It provides expertise and support to local authorities to embed preparing for adulthood from the earliest years for all young people with special needs and supports schools with Educational Health and Care Planning around the four key outcomes of

- employment;
- friends, relationship and community;

- ▨ independent living; and

- ▨ good health.

Although PfA does emphasise "good health, friendships, relationships and community inclusion" (para. 3), arguably, it is less focused on the specific needs of young people with PMLD for similar reasons we saw earlier in public policy as it aims to ensure that young people with special needs "achieve paid employment and independent living" (para. 3)

As we will see in Part II, many individual schools all around the world have, of course, also developed exciting and innovative frameworks, provision and, in some cases, whole curricula to support young people with PMLD. Arguably, this has been encouraged within policy since at least 2006 when the UK government allowed for children with PMLD to be disapplied from all or part of the National Curriculum and associated assessment arrangements "to make an individual pupil's curriculum more appropriate to his or her needs" (DfES, 2006, p. 3). Nearly 90 schools in the UK also use some or all of the 'pre-formal' curriculum developed by the charity Equals (www.equals.co.uk) specifically for learners with PMLD, which is a 'holistic' approach which gives wellbeing, independence and social relationships equal status as other parts of the curriculum. One of the UK schools which has successfully developed its own provision is the school we focus on in Part III: Chailey Heritage School in Sussex, a non-maintained, Ofsted awarded 'Outstanding' special school for children and young people, aged 3 to 19, some who have profound and multiple learning difficulties. Its CHILD (Chailey Heritage Individual Learner Driven) curriculum is centred on the child themselves and prioritises long-term outcomes which include social and emotional wellbeing, independence and community involvement.

So now it is time to move on from research literature and policy and towards actual school practice to support the wellbeing and independence of young people with PMLD. In Part II, we are going to hear the voices of hundreds of teachers, learning support assistants, parents, carers and a whole host of other practitioners who gave their time so generously to respond to the *Lives Lived Well* international surveys.

40 Part I

Reference list

Anand, D. (2016). *Happiness, well-being and human development: The case for subjective measures* (Human Development Report Background Paper). New York: UNDP Human Development Report Office.

Bickenbach, J. (2014). Disability and the well-being agenda. In J. Bickenbach, F. Felder, & B Schmitz (Eds.), *Disability and the good human life* (pp. 168–198). Cambridge: Cambridge University Press.

Burch, L. (2017). The governmentality of adulthood: A critical discourse analysis of the 2014 special educational needs and disability code of practice. *Disability and Society*. doi:10.1080/09687599.2017.1383231

Catlin, N. (2018). Having a road map for life: Creating an educational health and care plan for Duchenne muscular dystrophy. In J. Hoskin (Ed.) *A guide to Duchene muscular dystrophy* (pp. 139–163). London: Jessica Kingsley Publishers.

Department of Health. (2001). *Valuing people.* London: Her Majesty's Government / Department of Health.

Department of Health. (2007). *Aiming high for disabled children.* Her Majesty's Government / Department of Health.

Department of Health. (2009). *Valuing people now: A new three-year strategy for people with learning disabilities.* London: Her Majesty's Government / Department of Health.

Dept. for Education and Skills. (2006). *Disapplication of the national curriculum* (Rev. ed.). London: HMSO.

DfE. (2015). *Special educational needs and disability code of practice: 0–25 years.* London: HMSO.

Doukas, T., Fergusson, A., Fullerton, M., & Grace, J. (2017). *Supporting people with profound and multiple learning disabilities: Core and essential service standards.* PMLD Link.

The Electoral Commission. (2019). *Application to vote by proxy based on disability.* Retrieved from www.electoralcommission.org.uk/sites/default/files/2019-09/Disability-proxy-vote-application-form.pdf

Gauthier-Boudreault, C., Beaudoin, A., Gallagher, F., & Couture, M. (2017). Scoping reviews of social participation of individuals with profound intellectual disability in adulthood: What can I do once I finish school? *Journal of Intellectual and Developmental Disability, 19*(2), 248–260.

Hewett, D. (2018). *The intensive interaction handbook* (2nd ed.) London: Sage.

Hill, A. (2020, June 11). Court overturns 'right to sex' ruling on man who cannot understand consent. *The Guardian Newspaper.* Retrieved from www.theguardian.com/law/2020/jun/11/court-overturns-right-to-sex-ruling-on-man-who-cannot-understand-consent

Hoskin, J. (Ed.). (2018). *A guide to Duchene muscular dystrophy*. London: Jessica Kingsley Publishers.

Imray, P., & Colley, A. (2017). *Inclusion is dead. Long live inclusion*. London: Routledge.

Johnson, K., & Walmsley, J. (2010.). *People with intellectual disabilities. Towards a good life?* Bristol: The Policy Press.

Jordan, R. (2013). *Autism with severe learning difficulties* (2nd ed.). London: Souvenir Press.

Nind, M., & Strnadova, I. (2020). Changes in the lives of people with PIMD. In M. Nind & I. Strnadova (Eds.), *Belonging for people with profound intellectual and multiple disabilities* (pp. 1–21). London: Routledge.

Nussbaum, M. C. (2007). *Frontiers of justice – Disability, nationality, species membership*. Cambridge, MA: Harvard University Press.

Nussbaum, M. C. (2010). The capabilities of people with cognitive disabilities. In E. F. Kittay & L. Carlson (Eds.), *Cognitive disability and its challenge to moral philosophy* (pp. 75–95). Oxford: John Wiley Blackwell.

OECD. (2011). *How's life? Measuring well-being*. OECD Publishing. Retrieved from http://dx.doi.org/10.1787/9789264121164-en

Office for Standards in Education Ofsted). (2019). *The education inspection framework – Framework for inspections carried out, respectively, under section 5 of the Education Act 2005 (as amended), section 109 of the education and skills act 2008, the education and inspections act 2006 and the childcare act 2006*. London: Her Majesty's Stationary Office.

Ouvry, C. (1987). *Educating children with profound handicaps*. Kidderminster: BIMH Publications.

Palikara, O., Castro, S., Gaona, C., & Vasiliki, E. (2018). Capturing the voices of children in the EHC plans: Are we there yet? *Frontiers in Education, 3*(24). doi:10.3389/feduc.2018.00024

Preparing for Adulthood. (2020). Retrieved from www.preparingforadulthood. org.uk/

Public Health England. (2019). *All our health – About the framework*. Retrieved from www.gov.uk/government/publications/all-our-health-about-the-framework/all-our-health-about-the-framework

Shah, H., & Marks, N. (2014). *A well-being manifesto for a flourishing society*. London: The New Economics Foundation.

Shakespeare, T. (2014). *Disability rights and wrongs* (2nd ed.). London: Routledge.

Stiglitz, J., & United Nations. Commission of Experts on the Reform of the International Financial Monetary System. (2009). *The Stiglitz report: Reforming the international monetary and financial systems in the wake of the global crisis*. London: New Press.

UNICEF. (2002). *A world fit for children*. New York: UNICEF.

United Nations. (1989). *Convention on the rights of the child (UNCRC)*. Retrieved from www.unicef.org.uk/what-we-do/un-convention-child-rights/

United Nations. (2007). *Convention on the rights of persons with disabilities (CRPD)*. Retrieved from www.un.org/development/desa/disabilities/convention-on-the-rights-of-persons-with-disabilities.html

World Health Organisation (WHO). (2018). *Mental health: Strengthening our response*. Geneva: World Health Organisation Retrieved from www.who.int/news-room/fact-sheets/detail/mental-health-strengthening-our-response

PART II

5 An introduction to the *Lives Lived Well* surveys

One of the aims of this book is to present a rich and positive picture of practice in schools around the world and to share that practice with other practitioners, but also to discuss common barriers experienced by schools who work with learners with profound and multiple learning difficulties (PMLD). As far as we are aware, the *Lives Lived Well* UK and international surveys are the first attempt for at least 10 years to paint a picture of practice in and beyond school around the world with young people with PMLD. Previously to this, the Spring 2010 edition of *PMLD Link Magazine* (Vol 22, No. 1, Issue 65) was devoted to 'International Perspectives' and contained articles by practitioners from some of the countries represented by the *Lives Lived Well* international surveys – Ireland, Kenya, Australia and Israel, as well as Crete, Japan and Peru, and it is certainly worth tracking down a copy for the fascinating insight into perspectives and practice around the world at that time.

The UK survey

The *Lives Lived Well* UK survey, and in a way this book itself, began life in November 2018 at a conference organised by Flo Longhorn at Swiss Cottage School in London for about 80 practitioners in the field of PMLD education. One of our authors, Andrew Colley, stood at the front of the hall and simply asked practitioners to write down what they felt the burning issues were at that time around learners with PMLD.

46 Part II

'Wellbeing', expressed in different ways, was top of the list of concerns, with some of the other more detailed responses as follows:

I worry that my pmld pupils are not able to access the community.
In my experience in 3 schools, pupil voice is not accessed at all.
There is inconsistency about what 'independence' means.
Is the local community encouraged to engage with pupils with pmld?

Crucially, one respondent, a special school headteacher, wrote that although the *Special Education Needs and Disabilities (SEND) Code of Practice* (2015) appears to 'cover' learners with PMLD, they felt that at the same time it may not 'cater' for them, and we discuss this discrepancy again more fully in Chapter 9.

We realised at that point that there were some big questions that needed answering and so as part of a Master's by Research with the Cambridge University Faculty of Education, and after much thought, testing, piloting and re-piloting, the UK-wide *Lives Lived Well* online survey was born. You can see the full version of both the UK and international questionnaires at the back of this book.

Between November 2019 and March 2020, participants from 52 of the approximately 207 schools in England and Wales who are authorised to teach young people with PMLD responded to the online questionnaire, and four people from these schools took part in a subsequent online focus group which explored and discussed issues raised in the questionnaire in more depth. The UK questionnaire was angled, although not exclusively, towards learners with PMLD in the 14–19 age range which represented on average 9% of each school's total cohort. Responses came in from teachers in all the administrative regions of England, as well as from Wales and one from Scotland, with the vast majority at 94% coming from day-only or residential special schools, although there were also single responses from a special provision in a mainstream school and a further education college. Nearly 19,000 words of raw data were gathered from free-text survey questions and posts to the online forum, as well as quantitative data in the form of graphs and tables, a few of which we reproduce in this book.

The international survey

The *Lives Lived Well* international survey, which ran from June to July 2020, generated 66 responses from the following 19 countries, with the number of responses from each country in brackets: Spain (15), Singapore (14), India (7), Israel (7), Thailand (5), the US (3), Australia (2), Finland (2) and 1 each from Cyprus, France, Greece, Hungary, Ireland, Kenya, Macedonia, Norway, Slovakia, Taiwan and Timor Leste.

The large number of responses from some countries compared to others was largely due to the hard work of people in these countries who took it on themselves to distribute the survey more widely than we would ever have been able to from our base in the UK. In particular, we owe a great debt of thanks to Prithvi Perepa, who seemed to pull a very large number of strings in India and especially in New Delhi, and the exceptional response rate from practitioners in Spain was thanks to the dedication and support of María Carrasco Galdó, who took it on herself to translate the survey into Spanish. The survey was also particularly popular in Singapore thanks to the efforts of Jimson Tham of the Rainbow Centre and Gena Tan Li Xin of the Cerebral Palsy Alliance School.

The international survey differed slightly from the original UK survey because, first and foremost, the UK survey was simply too long! Other differences included the use of 'convenience' and 'snowball' sampling, which meant that the survey was distributed informally from one colleague to another or through word of mouth. This also meant that we were unable to specifically target teachers or other school-based practitioners, which resulted in a much wider representation of the various people involved in the life of a young person with PMLD than in the UK. These included not only teachers and school leaders but also speech and language therapists, physiotherapists, psychologists, social workers, researchers, advisors, teacher trainers and parents. In terms of the content of the international questionnaire, we did not specify an age range for the pupils in the way we did with the UK survey. Also, and after much discussion amongst the authors of this book, it was decided not to include a dedicated question about sexual expression in order to acknowledge potential ethical or cultural issues in raising this subject in some countries.

48 Part II

Of course, and as we discuss later in this book, there tended to be a wider range of educational provision represented in the international responses compared to the UK, where most of the respondents worked in special schools. Amongst the international responses, only 37% of pupils with PMLD were educated in special schools, 19% in a special provision or class within a mainstream or general school, 13% in special schools on the same campus as mainstream schools, 10% were educated in a mainstream classroom alongside their 'mainstream' peers, 11% at a residential provision and the rest in a variety of provisions including being homeschooled, in private foster homes, not attending any education provision at all or, as one respondent put it darkly, 'in institutions'.

What was particularly encouraging and gratifying was to find that wellbeing and independence as concepts are clearly a primary concern for all the schools surveyed, and this is evidenced perhaps not only by the number of responses to the survey and the volume of data in those responses but also by the following comments recorded at the end of the questionnaire where respondents were asked if they had any further thoughts around the issues raised:

> I am glad that at last we are looking into this in terms of research. Well-being should be at the forefront of our thinking.
>
> This is a very valid subject to research.
>
> Very interesting and valid questions posed which merit more attention.
>
> I am glad someone is looking into this.
>
> Great to hear that such a study is being done.
>
> Thank you that studies about the real needs of people with pmld are being carried out. People with pmld are a "forgotten" collective and a lot of times "unknown" in the SEN [special educational needs] field.

And one headteacher from a school in Spain said very gratifyingly, "Your book will help a thousand of children and their families".

So now, over the next four chapters, we hear the voices of all those practitioners from the UK and around the world and, in some cases, the voices of the young people themselves as we reveal the results of the *Lives Lived Well* international surveys 2020.

Reference list

DfE. (2015). *Special educational needs and disability code of practice: 0–25 years.* London: HMSO.

PMLD Link. (2010). *PMLD Link Magazine, 22*(1), 65.

The *Lives Lived Well* surveys
Wellbeing

Introduction

This chapter presents the results of the *Lives Lived Well* UK and international surveys with respect to wellbeing. After some discussion, we decided to define *wellbeing* in a very general way as follows at the start of the questionnaire:

> There are many definitions of 'wellbeing' but for the purposes of this questionnaire we are defining wellbeing very broadly as being comfortable, healthy and happy.

The results show the many imaginative and effective ways schools all around the world are working to enhance the wellbeing of their students with profound and multiple learning difficulties (PMLD), but we also report on some of the barriers and issues they face trying to do this. In line with the definition offered to the respondents, we look in particular at not only how the physical and emotional wellbeing of pupils is supported but also how schools encourage their pupils to take full part in the school and local communities.

Of course, independence is also an important part of wellbeing, and as we saw in Part I, is often conflated with wellbeing in literature and policy. This is reflected very much in the responses given by schools who frequently mention independence as being key to the wellbeing of their learners. One UK respondent for instance describes how they address their pupils' "independence and self-confidence in school, beyond school and when they eventually leave school" as a core element of their wellbeing, and this is a sentiment echoed by a teacher from Israel, who writes that "physical therapy will also help them reach some level of independence". We have decided, however, to focus more specifically on independence in the next chapter and on all the work schools are doing to enhance independence, including how they listen to the voices of the young people in whatever form those voices take, as well as on as the role of family or carers in their lives. This chapter, however, is very simply and as far as possible about wellbeing.

Wellbeing at the heart of school practice

Interestingly, it is a teacher from Singapore who is one of the only practitioners across the more than 100 responses to the *Lives Lived Well* UK and international surveys who goes as far as to suggest an alternative definition of *wellbeing* for this group of students, putting forward "self-fulfilment", although, of course, as one of the UK respondents points out very clearly, all schools and practitioners do "think very carefully about what wellbeing means for people with pmld. It might look different for each person and be different from what a person without a disability views as wellbeing". This respondent to the survey has really struck at the heart here of what this book and this chapter, in particular, is all about – showing the range of individualised approaches to wellbeing adopted by schools to support each young person, because in nearly all the UK schools surveyed – and from most of the international respondents, we hear that wellbeing is very definitely at the heart of the provision for these students. In Finland, for instance, a researcher tells us that student wellbeing has to be embedded in the general education plan for young people with PMLD, and in Singapore, the government "encourages organisations or individuals to come forward to provide recreational activities for the individual pupil's wellbeing". Less formally perhaps, a learning support assistant in Thailand explains that in their school, they "always have a special project that relates to wellbeing", and writing from Spain, the parent of a child with PMLD tells us from the heart that their child's "teachers truly care about the wellbeing of their pupils".

Around the world, wellbeing is almost always approached in a 'personalised' way, and more than one UK teacher even uses the gentle term *bespoke*, evoking as it does the image of a tailor carefully fitting fine suits for customers of different shapes and sizes: suits they will feel comfortable in, suits which will make them feel good about themselves, suits which will maybe give them a feeling of 'self-fulfilment'.

This, of course, takes extraordinary skill, attention to detail and hard work on the part of the many teachers and other practitioners we hear from in the surveys, and if the *Lives Lived Well* project has shown anything, it is that around the world, teachers and other practitioners are always prepared to work as hard as they can to make sure each individual learner with PMLD has a provision which suits them. How exactly this is achieved is described by respondents in a number of ways, as we will see later, but most frame it as in one way or another as responding to their strengths and interests. One of the UK respondents echoes the ethos of Chailey Heritage School in Sussex, which we visit in Part III, by stating simply that the "child is the curriculum", and we hear the same message again and again around the world, with this from a teacher in Spain: "We try to pay attention to our students to learn about their needs, likes and preferences" and the following from a lead teacher in Massachusetts:

> We treat each student as an individual with individual needs, wants and preferences; we respect the students' moods, likes and dislikes.

Not surprisingly perhaps, this very individualised approach is central to the program described by a teaching assistant in a Steiner/Waldorf School in Hungary:

> Focus is given [to] each child's personality, reactions, strengths, areas of possible developments, likes, dislikes. We try to help the child to become the person who he or she wants to be.

There are no mentions in the UK surveys at all of the National Curriculum and very few of external curricula, and even when they are referred to, it is clear that schools, in the words of one respondent, "differentiate learning objectives, activities, timings and resources for each individual within the lesson". We already mentioned in Chapter 5 that formalised curricula or versions of a 'national curriculum' tend to be used more with this group in countries where 'full inclusion' is still favoured and where learners with PMLD work alongside peers in mainstream settings, and we discuss this in more detail later. In the UK, at least, however, special schools seem to be finally breaking away from the obligation to fit their learners with PMLD into some kind of one size fits all academic curriculum, be it the Early Years Foundations Stage or the National Curriculum itself in order to ensure that first and foremost it is the comfort and wellbeing of each pupil which at the heart of the agenda and not an externally imposed and assessed programme of study. In fact, we sometimes forget that this has been possible in the UK at least since 2006 when schools could apply for their learners to be 'disapplied' from the National Curriculum, but the reality is that some schools initially shied away from doing this, often perhaps because of the results-driven culture some writers and researchers touched on in Part I as being a poor match for learners with PMLD.

Where pre-existing curriculum content or strategies are used, they tend to be described as "broad and balanced" (DfE, 2015, p. 94), which is in line with the guidance contained in the *Special Educational Needs and Disabilities (SEND) Code of Practice* (2015) or are ones with personalisation and wellbeing as their central tenets such as multisensory activities and, in particular, Intensive Interaction (Hewett, 2018) which engages with the child on their terms and when they are ready and which is mentioned by many respondents in the UK and also seems to be widely used in Australia.

Getting to know you

With the wellbeing of the young person at the centre of what we might still call the 'curriculum', the key first step is getting to know that young person as well as possible, with approaches ranging from simply observing: "We look and listen very closely to the young person" to ones based more closely on building relationships, as here from the UK surveys:

> We closely get to know the students on a personal level so that we can identify their individual signals, however great or small.
> We build up great relationships with pupils so that we understand their responses, sounds, facial expressions etc.
> Understanding who they are and allowing their personalities to shine.

For some practitioners, getting to know the learner means also engaging closely with the home, with teachers in Singapore for instance conducting

> mandatory home visits so that they can find out more about the needs of the students within the home. Teachers work closely with family members to find out more about the needs of the students so as to ensure that the students are comfortable and well taken care of in school.

This is emphasised also in responses from Finland and France and from a teacher in Spain: "it is important to record the information from their families from the home context". This key issue of the role of the parents and carers is one we discuss more fully in Chapter 7 when we look more closely at independence.

Readiness for learning, often framed as "making the moment count", "going with the incidental moments of learning", "opening their world to connections" or as described by a teacher in Singapore "students learning at their own pace", is at the heart of this personalisation process, and in some cases, lessons "only begin when pupils are ready to learn", showing that many schools are prepared to challenge the traditional structure of the school day and adopt a flexible timetable with respect to pupils with PMLD in order to make sure that each pupil's wellbeing is prioritised. In Finland, for instance, "schools have lots of flexibility and autonomy to organize their work", and a lead teacher in Massachusetts ensures that she "makes schedules that are flexible so students who are having a hard time can have a break and then go back to working". The vast majority of responses then show that, as a physiotherapist from Spain makes clear, "every person receives an individual treatment, no one is considered the same as someone else".

Sadly, however, there are reports from respondents in a small number of countries that the wellbeing of learners with PMLD is not always as central to provision as it perhaps should be or is elsewhere, and we are careful here not to name these countries specifically. An advisor working with schools in a number of countries explains that "there is no provision or support for these young people and no monitoring in place to be able to assess their wellbeing", and a key worker from an East African country states bluntly that "there is no emphasis on wellbeing", although qualifies that to some extent by explaining that "as long as their primary needs for food, clothing and shelter are looked after I think that is what counts as their wellbeing here". This emphasis on primary needs is also found in this response from another key worker, this time in South-East Asia: "I'm not sure if they are emotionally comfortable, healthy and happy, but physically, they are provided with good meals". In the next section then, we start by finding out what schools around the world do to support the physical wellbeing of this group before moving on to their equally important emotional wellbeing.

Physical wellbeing

Returning though to the definition of *wellbeing* offered to respondents at the start of the *Lives Lived Well* survey, responses to the UK questionnaire show that it is ensuring they are comfortable and healthy or, in other words, their physical wellbeing, which is primarily supported and addressed within the busy school day, although as we have said before physical wellbeing and emotional wellbeing are, of course, not two separate things and, as one UK respondent puts it, "repositioning promotes wellbeing". As we will see later, the emotional wellbeing of the pupils is by no means ignored, but there is a clear sense, however, that in a school day, what one respondent calls the "work we do to ensure pupils are as comfortable as possible" takes priority. In some respects, this is inevitable in view of the time and resources required to support the physical wellbeing of someone with complex physical needs, and as teachers, we are sure that we have all felt at times that at the end of a long school day it can seem that this is all we have done.

To explore this balance between physical and emotional wellbeing further, the international survey (see Figure 6.1) asked directly whether schools supported the emotional wellbeing and the physical wellbeing of this group equally, and the results show that they do in fact do both.

Support for physical wellbeing in whatever form will always be part of the lives of many of these young people, and so it makes perfect sense that it will also be a big part of their daily school provision. If each young person carries within them their own curriculum, then physical support, personal care and repositioning aren't inconvenient extras in a busy school day. They are part of the personalisation process, and without these, their wellbeing cannot be assured.

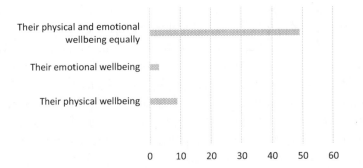

Figure 6.1 International survey: Which of the following is prioritized in your school or setting with respect to young people with PMLD?

The list of activities across the 52 UK schools and from the 66 international practitioners to ensure their pupils are physically comfortable and healthy is long and impressive and based again on close knowledge and understanding of each individual young person, as expressed here:

> We become familiar with the signs that they communicate that let you know they may be uncomfortable in some way, then work through the things that could be causing this.

These physical activities can be simply "getting out of their wheelchairs" and "time out of wheelchairs", "providing postural management throughout the day" or, in the words of a speech and language therapist (SaLT) from Singapore, "ensuring an optimal seating position", with more than one school insisting on a minimum number of positional changes per day and another building variety even into this process by showing that positional changes take place "on mats, in standers, walkers etc". More than half the respondents mention physiotherapy, and for some, "every day has an element of physiotherapy", with a physiotherapist from Spain giving us an insight into the care taken to get things just right:

> The work of physiotherapy is integrated in the classroom, with postural treatments, distribution of spaces appropriate to each user, positioning material (adapted chairs, adapted tables) individualized in the classroom.

There are physical education (PE) lessons, occupational therapy, reflexology, use of standing frames and yoga offered in more than one school in New Delhi, India. There is also extensive use of some commercially developed programmes, such as Rebound Therapy (www.reboundtherapy.org), the MOVE programme (www.enhamtrust.org.uk/move-programme-subsite) and Emmett Therapies (www.emmett-uk.co.uk/) mentioned in the UK and Basale Stimulation (www.basale-stimulation.de), Kinaesthetics and Bobath Therapy (www.bobath.org.uk) used in a number of schools in Spain.

Many schools in the UK and elsewhere enjoy the benefits of warm-water therapy pools and hydrotherapy sessions, and swimming in general is a popular activity mentioned by many of our international respondents, with a teacher from Cyprus enthusing about the added benefit of the climate:

> They take advantage of the weather (which is beautiful) most year-round and they tend to take them for swimming or walks etc.

Perhaps hinting darkly, however, at some of the logistical or financial issues faced by schools, a couple of the UK respondents point out that much of this activity depends on "specialised equipment such as portable hoists, seating, wheelchairs, bespoke manual handling equipment" as well as bikes, "all terrain wheelchairs", standing frames and the ACHEEVA beds mentioned by a number of respondents, but having to "buy and maintain a range of equipment for postural care" places a significant financial burden on schools.

Importantly, some of the schools in the UK do acknowledge that being the receiver of postural management can compromise a young person's wellbeing and, in particular, with respect to their independence or dignity and are aware of the dangers for the young people of having routines carried out on them and so take care to "allow them to know what's happening and to let them lead" with staff "who will 'do with' rather than 'do to' our young people with dignity, care, compassion and empathy". Many schools around the world, of course, do employ what several refer to as "high ratios of trained staff", and this raises the key issue of the role of the staff supporting the learner with personal care whether it be one or sometimes even two people. We explore this in more detail in the next chapter and discuss to what extent fulfilment can be found in relationships of dependency such as these when the person with PMLD is dependent on another for physical care.

The physical wellbeing of the pupils is supported in many cases by a range of specialist staff including physiotherapists, occupational therapists, SaLTs and psychologists in more than one European country, as well, of course, as nurses and paediatricians. In this way, as one teacher in Singapore explains "everybody learns from the other and has knowledge of what is needed by the pupil in every other area. Thus, each staff can implement strategies which is not under their expertise". Very few schools, however, have the "trained children's nurses on site" or the extensive provision described by two of the UK residential schools:

> A full clinical team of SaLT, physio, Occupational Therapists and nursing.
> A full team of on-site therapists.

For some schools, this kind of support comes in the form of "nursing advice", which is usually "weekly", as well as some training to staff around medical and other issues, including "health, diet, eye sight and dental care", "respiratory therapies", "wheelchair, orthotics, paediatrician, emergency epilepsy medication, enteral feeding, and managing tracheostomy etc". The reality, however, seems to be that in most special schools that do not have residential provision, it falls to the "highly skilled classroom practitioners" to deliver the day-to-day medical and care needs which support the wellbeing of young people with PMLD or, in other words, the teachers and teaching assistants, and many teachers will recognise these comments from teachers in Israel: "It is our staff who have to keep on top of all of the students' health problems and needs . . . we provide them with three meals a day and hygienic care including bathing and care for teeth".

Not surprisingly then, respondents to the questionnaires – often people in leadership positions in the schools – are fulsome in their praise of their staff, not only describing them, of course, as "well-trained" and "highly skilled" but also highlighting their personal qualities and attributes variously described as "supportive and caring", "caring and enabling", "understanding", "loving" and as people "who will listen to them, encourage them and never give up". It is these same staff, of course, who also undertake on a daily basis what is referred to most usually by respondents as 'personal 'or 'intimate' care and the impact of this on their independence raises further important issues which we discuss in the next chapter.

Emotional wellbeing

The staff then are also key to supporting the pupils to achieve the third element of the definition of 'wellbeing' suggested to respondents at the start of the questionnaire: 'being happy' because, as one respondent put it, "allowing staff to spend time discovering what makes pupils happy upholds their wellbeing", and in one of the most memorable phrases amongst all the more than 100 responses to the UK and international surveys, a teacher in Spain summarised this with the phrase "the pedagogy of affection".

Hearteningly, amongst the responses in the wellbeing section of the UK questionnaire, there were six separate mentions of *fun*, seven of *play* or *playfulness* and nine of *happy* or *happiness*, with one school summing up its approach succinctly as an "ethos to have fun", echoing Johnson, Douglas, Bigby, and Iacono' (2012) conclusion that laughter in social situations is positive for both communication partners, and this is very much reflected in responses from practitioners all around the world with many references to "fun and engaging activities", such as music, art therapy, animal therapy and a school in Israel using what the teacher describes delightfully as "snoozland therapy", which is almost certainly a reference to the multisensory approach usually called 'snoezelen' (www.snoezelen.info). We also get this wonderfully evocative picture of life in the classroom in Spain from a speech and language specialist: "games, dancing, hugging, eye-contact, and just speaking to them", with a teacher in Massachusetts pointing out that it is important that it is not just the students who deserve to have fun:

> We incorporate fun and creative teaching into lessons so that both the students and the staff are enjoying themselves.

We saw in Part I that 'mental health' is a key element of 'wellbeing' and that rates of mental illness are higher for those with all learning difficulties than in the general population and even higher for those with profound needs (Bouras, Hardy, & Holt, 2011), and we discussed why mental illness in this group is difficult to diagnose and treat. Possibly reflecting these challenges, there are only a few specific mentions of 'mental health' within the responses to the UK survey, although three schools routinely undertake 'happiness audits', with one school currently in the process of becoming a "trauma and mental health informed school". There is, however, a clear sense that the mental health of young people with PMLD in schools all around the world is first and foremost addressed by providing what an Israeli teacher describes as "a warm and safe environment", with "respectful and supportive staff who provide for their physical and emotional needs" which can be simply "recognising when they need a break" as emphasised by a deaf/blind specialist in Ireland, and these more all-encompassing approaches from teachers in Thailand and Singapore:

> We help our pupils understand and realize wellbeing in their own lives.
> We ensure that school is a safe place for them, give them a sense of belonging and happiness in coming to school to participate and learn.

Wellbeing, of course, goes beyond narrow definitions of physical and emotional wellbeing and the things which have an impact on our wellbeing come in many forms. In 2020, we all found out exactly how much community participation is vital to our wellbeing and when that is withdrawn – as it was when the world went into 'lockdown' – we discovered how important other people are to our feelings of wellbeing. So, taking a lead from some of the theory and research discussed in Part I, the *Lives Lived Well* surveys asked teachers and practitioners about the importance of community participation for young people with PMLD and about some of the barriers they face when trying to ensure these young people can take a full part in their school and local and wider communities.

Participation in the school community

This is not a book about 'inclusion', but it is the case in some countries that there is at least an assumption in both policy and practice that young people with PMLD will in some way or another be educated alongside their peers of all abilities – if not in the same classroom, then often in the same school – and in Chapter 9, we hear from teachers, parents, researchers and school leaders what they think about this and whether they feel whatever form of 'inclusion' is practised in their country works for young people with PMLD.

With respect to the data gathered from the *Lives Lived Well* internationals survey, however, only one respondent, a researcher from Finland, seemed to suggest that some form of 'full inclusion' in mainstream schools is practised in their country with respect to this cohort:

> According to the latest research those pupils who study in mainstream school attend to all common activities (breaks, lunch time, celebrations). And some (not many) attend also subject lessons (music, PE, home economics, arts).

Most of the international responses that address this issue do, however, point towards a closer relationship with mainstream schools than we perhaps see in the UK, as with this response from an occupational therapist in New York state: "They are included in mainstream activities as much as possible – for e.g. assemblies and specials." This seems to be particularly the case in Spain, where, in one school in Alicante, the pupils

> have their schedule and materials to attend a mainstream classroom, joining them when they go out, attending tutorials, extracurriculars, sports club. . . . When necessary, they are supported at these times by teachers, speech therapists or learning support assistants.

In another school, this time in Murcia, Spain, "we do inclusive activities to socialise with mainstream students and call it inclusive leisure. We also have shared playgrounds with other mainstream schools so they can meet with each other and realise there are not many differences between them". Commonly then, these 'inclusive' activities are social events or what is often referred to as 'seasonal events' such as carnivals, outings, sports days and drama activities.

So when we talk in this chapter about participation in the school community, it is important to note that in the UK this almost always means in the community of a special school, whereas in other coun-

62 Part II

tries, this may be the perhaps larger community of a mainstream or 'regular' school.

For many then, it is first and foremost successful participation in the school community which is essential to the wellbeing of these young people, more so often than the provision of the timetabled 'community activities' which take them out of school and which we discuss later. One of the special schools which responded to the *Lives Lived Well* survey from the UK, listed some of the many benefits which come from involving their learners with PMLD in their own school community and that of a nearby mainstream school because "all pupils have equal value":

> Meaningful, authentic, mutually beneficial friendships with children who do not have PMLD.
> Pupils with PMLD sharing core experiences alongside children of their own age who themselves have a wide range of learning needs.
> Becoming one 'Family Group'.
> Participating in weekly whole class inclusion sessions in mainstream settings.
> Breaking down social barriers.
> Promoting the expectation that people with PMLD can demonstrate independence when given the chance.

This multilayered community ethos is echoed by a lead teacher from Massachusetts, who writes that "even partial participation is valuable to the community as a whole" and another in Australia who talks of the key importance of "contact with friendship groups" for the wellbeing of pupils with PMLD.

Typically, schools around the world encourage full participation of these young people in all aspects of school life as witnessed in these testimonies from the UK, Spain, Thailand and Singapore:

> Students participate in all aspects of the school social life from lunchtime clubs to whole school events such as the Christmas Bazaar.
> Activities and workshops are organised in which all students participate . . . and we do extra activities with a big group to encourage social relationships with their peers (going to the cinema, welcoming first day all together, adapted sports days. . .). We prepare interactive activities for the big events: Christmas, Carnival, Easter,

and '*Fallas*', a local festivity where a cardboard monument is burnt. We also do school journeys with a two-night overnight stay at an adapted camping or hostel.

We always ensure pupils with pmld are involved in all activities.

There are communication opportunities to send messages to other classrooms using AAC [augmented and alternative communication] devices.

There is also clear evidence from the UK at least that the students with PMLD participate in school council, and in that school in Cyprus, when they are not out enjoying the sun, "they cook for the whole class: breakfast for example", whilst residential schools, in particular, are in a position to provide opportunities for creating a rich community such as this one in the UK:

We have a range of facilities that are shared by our pupils and over 90 adults with PMLD and the opportunity for social interaction amongst themselves are great.

Very occasionally, schools mention "peer support" for learners with PMLD, and although there are no details given in the questionnaires, our own experience working in special schools in the UK has shown that in some settings pupils with mild to moderate learning difficulties do support learners with PMLD in practical ways such as by pushing wheelchairs and through various 'buddying' systems, although schools leaders can be reluctant to do this unless very rigorous risk assessments can be carried out. In some cases, as in this school in Singapore "older students from a nearby (mainstream) school come to us to teach the younger students", and in a setting in Israel,

twice a week there are neurotypical peers that come over to our school and they have a lesson together, they get to know each other, learn how our students communicate etc. Also, their brothers and sisters come a few times a year to what we call 'siblings activity'.

To explore the issue of peer support further in the UK context, it was addressed subsequently in a post in the UK online focus group, and the responses seem to frame peer support as more commonly an opportunity for socialisation:

All of our pupils with PMLD work and socialise with their peers of all types and levels of learning difficulty within the school. We group our pupils by age rather than ability, and so pupils with PMLD learn to work and participate in [the] community with a small group of 7 or 8 other children of their own age in mixed ability lessons every day. Additionally, every class spends half a day a week joining a mainstream class of the same age in a local school, learning to learn together.

In general, then, the world over, these young people are very much part of school communities where they "feel safe and happy to be". However, one respondent sums up the feelings of many: "It's difficult both logistically and practically to bridge the gap between school and the outside world", with one teacher in Spain calling for more "community support for families to go out with their sons and daughters". This concern is evidenced by the fact that an overwhelming 80% of respondents in the UK survey (see Figure 6.2) either mostly or completely agree that '*the social life of someone with PMLD is largely focused on their family or school*'.

This feeling was backed up to a certain extent in the international survey where nearly half the respondents completely or mostly agreed that the families of people with PMLD live isolated lives, although that

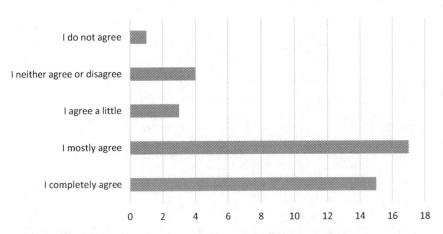

Figure 6.2 To what extent do you agree that *the* social life of someone with PMLD is largely focused on their family or school?

was mitigated to a certain extent in some countries by a greater involvement from the wider family, as mentioned by a teacher in Greece:

> There is usually a good family and friends support systems and the families of people with pmld do not feel isolated.

Participation in the wider community beyond school

Schools do, of course, however, try to bridge that gap, and most, if not all, include some kind of timetabled activity which is described variously as "visits into the community", "access to the wider community" or, in Thailand, for instance, "special occasions in communities", although as one teacher in Australia reminds us we must be careful not to impose trips and visits on young people especially when they are old enough to choose: "community participation is not always what the students want".

Nevertheless, in general, there are programmes of community walks and visits to shops, cafes, museums and parks as well as some more ambitious projects such as "community trips to local businesses and fundraising events" in Ireland and, in Singapore, what sounds like quite a complex project "with corporate partners, volunteers and other schools/institutions". There are also special events which in one UK case intriguingly is "filming for the Christmas Film at local locations". The rationale for these community activities is framed in a number of ways as follows:

> Becoming valued and valuable members of the community.
> Community learning and social interaction.
> Supporting pupils to apply learned communication skills to a broader context.
> To expose students to the community and allow [the] community to be exposed and educated about the PMLD community.
> We have found that these activities seem to make our students happy and this helps with inclusion too, as they feel they are a part of the community.

Addressing a very recent issue which has had an impact perhaps on this cohort more than most, one classroom assistant in Singapore laments the impact of the coronavirus pandemic on these types of community activity:

> Before Covid, we used to have combined lessons to create projects, even venturing out into the public, now we still do have projects going on but more within the school.

However, despite the efforts made by the schools to involve their pupils with PMLD in the local community in one way or another, the UK survey found that nearly 70% of pupils with PMLD do so less than their peers (see Figure 6.3). When a similar question was asked in the international survey, we get more or less the same picture (see Figure 6.4).

Two schools only in the UK indicated that their pupils with PMLD access the local community more than their peers. One is a special school with 43%, one of the largest percentages, of pupils with PMLD amongst its total school population and explains that it "work[s] hard to get out as it helps prepare students for future life". The other is one of the residential schools whose pupils "go out during the school day as part of the curriculum and beyond the school day if they are resident".

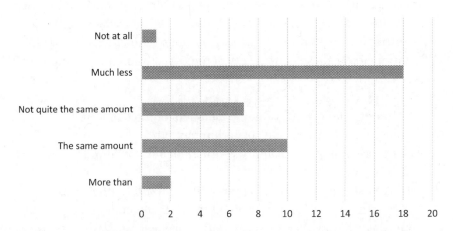

Figure 6.3 UK survey: On a scale of 1 to 5, with one being 'not at all' and 5 being 'more than,' to what extent do these learners access the community as part of their school provision at the same rate as those with less severe or complex levels of learning difficulty?

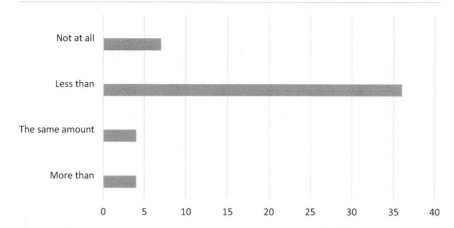

Figure 6.4 International survey: On a scale of 1 to 4, with one being 'not at all' and 4 being 'more than,' to what extent do these learners access the community as part of their school provision at the same rate as those with less severe or complex levels of learning difficulty?

Some schools take a pragmatic and even positive approach to this issue simply because often "preparing to go on a difficult to arrange trip to the shops and the work involved does not balance with what the pupils receive from the community facilities". *Not* going out on a community trip can make space for "bringing things into school for them" as well as "invaluable quiet times and one to one interactions, and creating a "circle of friends" or what one school summarises simply as "hanging out: time with things or people they enjoy". This echoes research discussed in Part I (e.g. Bellamy, Croot, Bush, Berry, & Smith, 2010, p. 232) that parents and carers prefer definitions of community which highlight "the circumstances which are necessary to enable individuals with pmld to be given the opportunity to participate in their immediate situation".

Schools give a number of reasons why their pupils with PMLD go out in the community less than their peers with milder or more moderate needs do. Predominantly, these are factors which are outside the school's control, and we look at those later, but some of the reasons were connected to the school provision itself, with several respondents citing staffing issues and the availability of drivers or suitably equipped minibuses, while a number of teachers around the world cite funding issues. For others, the planning, timetabling and other "organisational demands" involved can feel overwhelming, with one teacher in the international survey admitting, "We don't go out much; we leave it to the family".

Very often, the reasons for not going out are because of some of the pupils' "complex medical needs and all the equipment they require in order to stay safe", but other logistical issues need to be taken into account as well, particularly with respect to pupils who are wheelchair users, with a teacher in Spain commenting, "People with pmld who are wheelchair users need a person to go and to participate in each activity the community offers".

Organising a trip out is a fairly daunting task, and this small sample of the many comments we received on this issue will be all too familiar to anyone who has worked with this group of young people:

> There are challenges bringing all the equipment needed to spend a day [in] other settings.
> All outings need to be planned very carefully and a risk assessment must be completed before an outing can be agreed.
> Gathering and preparing all equipment takes a long time and requires a lot of space.
> We can only take two wheelchairs at a time.
> The time involved in clamping a group of pupils onto a minibus means short trips are difficult.

More pragmatically, however, a teacher in Israel explains that "young people with pmld are in school until the late afternoon and therefore don't go out much to the community", and one school in the UK offers this intriguingly simple explanation as to why pupils with PMLD go out less than others: "the rest of the school move faster than us".

Overall, however, schools around the world point to a deficiency in provision of resources and facilities out in the community, with one summing up the concerns simply as "community facilities need to be far better than they are" and public transport often cited as a particular issue. For several respondents, accessibility is often the key issue out in the local community, especially as "pmld wheelchairs can be very large and heavy" and footpaths and sidewalks are often perceived not to be

The *Lives Lived Well* surveys: wellbeing **69**

"suitable and safe", and there is also a particular problem with "the limited access to adequate spaces for personal care" or what is often referred to as 'changing places', with frustrations expressed around "access to appropriate facilities such as toilets for pmld students". These are concerns and issues clearly shared around the world, with a teacher complaining that in her country, "community participation is hard to achieve as there is no good provision for wheelchair users" and a key worker from East Africa telling us that "appropriate adjustments in buildings or public transportation are lacking. Wheelchairs are quite rigid and old-fashioned which do not allow easy manoeuvring in community settings", whilst in Israel, and quite understandably "some cities are old and therefore not accessible, although there have been improvements". In fact, it is actually encouraging to hear how much progress is being made around the world with accessibility, with respondents also from the US, Australia, Singapore and Spain all heralding improvements in public services for wheelchair users.

But setting aside issues of physical access and remembering that by no means all young people with PMLD use wheelchairs, one respondent remarks that "wheelchair accessible does not always mean pmld accessible" and another that there is a "lack of places to go that are better or the same as facilities at school". Clubs and societies are cited by six respondents as in short supply outside of school, and where they do exist, often they tend to cater for people with a specific condition, are simply "not equipped to provide the type of support required by these young people" or do not have "suitably trained staff/carers". Again, this has echoes around the world where, in various ways, community facilities and activities are said to be underfunded or not thought to be suitable for people with PMLD, although in Israel, community participation is "achieved through a small amount of programs as well as youth groups and camp programs but much more is needed".

Nor do families find it any easier to provide meaningful community experiences for their children with PMLD, because participation by a young person with PMLD is very much dependent on someone who is willing to "initiate that participation" whether that be simply leisure time such as "spending time outdoors, joining clubs and or having hobbies". Employing someone to do this is often compromised due to the hours and pay, with a teacher from Israel reminding us that for a lot of families "finding an appropriate and competent carer is difficult", especially when sometimes two people are required. A number of other respondents acknowledge the challenges faced by parents and carers, particularly when they have other children, as well as their "willingness" to organise access to activities themselves for the child with PMLD. "Families remain isolated", one UK teacher points out, "because of the difficulties getting out and about".

In general, respondents from the UK do not mention negative public attitudes towards people with PMLD as a barrier to community participation, although as we will see later, they are very aware of the need to raise awareness. Sadly, however, many responses to the international survey paint a different picture, and again, we have tried to be discreet about which countries these comments come from. Some explain that the lack of 'inclusion' in their country means that people with PMLD are less visible and therefore less understood:

> Because people with pmld learn in special schools, other people aren't exposed to them.
> They are kept away from their peers and communities under the guise of providing them one to one adult support as early as they attend school. After that it is very difficult to try to make them part of the community or society.
> Historically people with disabilities are hidden.

And on this topic, the parent of one young person is in no doubt that "changing mentalities takes a long time but from my personal experience having the pmld classrooms integrated to regular school is a huge game changer where children get to interact from an early age and are not biased by society".

For some, there is "an enormous amount of goodwill", but for others, the picture is bleaker, and again, we do not want to point the finger at certain countries, so in this short paragraph about social attitudes, we are not going to link any quotations we use to a particular respondent or to a particular country, especially as some of the attitudes described are quite upsetting for all of us who care about people with PMLD. Eight of the respondents to the international survey discuss what one calls the "ignorance of society" and another, the "very low levels of community understanding of disability". For some, this leads to a "difficulty for the community to understand how to interact with people with pmld", with fear put forward by several to explain this reluctance to engage with people with pmld. One baldly states that "people are afraid to interact with them". Nor was it unusual to find mentions of taboos around profound disability still in place in a number of countries, and in the examples that follow, we can see that these attitudes have a particularly negative effect on families and, in some cases, lead to them being as one describes it "shunned":

> Parents fear people's reaction in public settings. They feel isolated and pointed out.
> Special schools are shunned due to stigma.
> They sort of look down on them.
> Most families with people with pmld get stared at.
> Families fear what the neighbours or friends may say.
> Some families prefer to keep their situation private.

Some of the respondents put forward more nuanced explanations ranging from "different cultural values" to discussions about the extent to which society has already "stereotyped people with disabilities" and whether "neuro-typical people tend to sympathize instead of empathize" or "pity instead of support" this group of people, going on to say that "people do not understand that people with pmld have emotions and needs just like us all".

Schools are clearly, however, very willing themselves to work to overcome some of these barriers to community participation, and many do this at the highest level by "working with MPs and councils" and petitioning local authorities to develop "more accessible transport systems" or, at the very least, provide "safe footpaths". A parent in Spain, in fact, situates this as "a global issue where all members of the society, starting with government leaders, should take more action", whilst a researcher in Norway calls for far more "awareness in teacher education".

As one teacher puts it, "schools do their best but if society is not ready to accommodate the needs of these people, then the role of schools is limited". However, on a local level, the majority of respondents to the *Lives Lived Well Survey* place an emphasis on raising awareness and "trying to build understanding", and these are common themes around the world, although a couple do acknowledge that a possible mitigating factor for community participation was that the catchment areas "that surround special schools are big and so families involved in the same school can live many miles apart" or that "most of the schools are also not in the most accessible areas of the community".

Principal amongst the suggestions for raising awareness is simply "getting out there" because "just being seen makes a huge difference", and other similar suggestions include "having conversations", "building supportive community links" and simply "visibility", with the onus on schools themselves to "normalise our students being in the wider world".

Others see this more in terms of "breaking down the fears that can often be in place in the general public", challenging "intolerance in the general community" and similarly "challenging low expectations of participation", and this is a theme taken up in many of the international responses as in these examples from teachers in Ireland and Cyprus:

> We must showcase ability and not disability, and be present and not hidden.
> By strengthening the fact that people with pmld are still the same people as everyone else.

There is a lot of discussion around the benefits of links with mainstream schools on the community participation of learners with PMLD, although it is only really respondents from Finland again who frame this as a call for fuller inclusion:

> Schools should take a stand for having these pupils as part of the school community, have and teach pupils among their typically developing peers and make sure that pupils' participation reaches not only physical but also social and emotional dimension . . . schools should be for all.

Other than Finland, we do hear from an advisor to a number of countries across the Asia Pacific region that "the current strategic plan is to build capacity across the school system but I suspect that young people with pmld will be one of the last groups to be included".

In general, however, respondents in the UK favour "combining mainstream and SEN [special educational needs] schools in outside community events", which, as we saw earlier in this chapter, many UK schools strive to do, and this is an approach favoured also by many practitioners around the world:

> In my opinion the best way is to connect between children with pmld and neurotypical children. (Teacher, Israel)
> To become more involved in projects with mainstream schools. (Teacher, Spain)
> Participating in activities organised by the local council and other mainstream schools. (Parent, Spain)

Others speak of educating the wider community because "community understanding of these needs would make for a more inclusive environment" and do this by "sharing our practices and philosophies", with a teaching assistant in Hungary making the very valid point that "the philosophy of the school and teaching program matter" and a key worker in Thailand explaining that "if the school has clear and correct mindset, it would help to correct the perception of people in communities towards individuals with severe disabilities". Many try to share their ethos and practices by trying to bring the community into the school itself, with concrete examples or suggestions being "inviting local mainstream schools to be volunteers", "inviting mainstream children to SEN schools and vice versa" or simply "opening our doors" to the community around the school with further suggestions from respondents in Israel, Kenya and Norway:

> Inviting people without disabilities to visit the special schools.
> Organising open days where the public can come into.
> Focusing on partnerships with the community and local organisations.
> Working with more community partners to create opportunities for these students to go out more into the community.

To summarise this chapter then, the *Lives Lived Well* international surveys have shown that around the world, the physical and emotional wellbeing of young people with PMLD – that 'pedagogy of affection' we heard about earlier – is very much at the forefront of the work teachers and other practitioners are doing, although in a very few countries the support offered may not be as rigorous and in depth as it could be, and sometimes the "hard work and commitment" one UK teacher talks about is not always matched by outside agencies and local authorities. In particular, the participation of this group of people in the wider community beyond school is often inadequate or compromised by a lack of appropriate facilities and resources as well as by stigma in some parts of the world, although, of course, we must not at the same time forget the words of the Australian teacher we quoted earlier and be mindful that "community participation is not always what the students want".

In view of these issues, there is then perhaps a need to adopt a more nuanced interpretation of community participation for this group and its contribution to an individual's wellbeing, and we have already seen this with schools that try to create rich community experiences in their schools rather than putting themselves through the often fraught process of going out into the community. Significantly, one of the questions in the UK questionnaire asked schools to list the elements which they felt contributed to valid and meaningful community participation for this group and 'participation in the local community' came behind arguably less formalised concepts such as 'social networks', 'emotional attachments', 'having a sense of belonging' and 'relationships with a parent or personal assistant'. This reflects discussions in Part I about valuing relationships of dependency (Kittay, 2011) and leads us now to the next chapter, where we find out how schools support these young people, despite their high level of need, to be and to feel as independent as possible.

Reference list

Bellamy, G., Croot, L., Bush, A., Berry, H., & Smith, A. (2010). A study to define profound and multiple learning disabilities (PMLD). *Journal of Intellectual Disabilities, 14*(3), 221–235.

Bouras, N., Hardy, S., & Holt, G. (2011). *Mental health in intellectual disabilities: A reader* (4th ed.). Brighton: Pavilion.

DfE. (2015). *Special educational needs and disability code of practice: 0–25 years.* London: HMSO.

Hewett, D. (2018). *The intensive interaction handbook* (2nd ed.) London: Sage.

Johnson, H., Douglas, J., Bigby, C., & Iacono, T. (2012). Social Interaction with adults with severe intellectual disability: Having fun and hanging out. *Journal of Intellectual Disabilities*, *25*, 329–341.

Kittay, E. (2011). The ethics of care, dependence and disability. *Ratio Juris*, *24*(1), 49–58.

The *Lives Lived Well* surveys
Independence

Independence at the heart of everything

As we saw in Part I, what 'independence' might mean for this group of young people and how possible it is to achieve is sometimes contested. In fact, picking up on the discussion at the end of the previous chapter around the value of community participation for this group, one school leader from Australia suggests that "independence is less important than a prepared community".

However, whilst I am sure we would all agree with a researcher from Norway that "it is a challenge", the aim to promote "as much independence and autonomy as possible" and "in every way" is at the heart of the ethos of so many of the schools worldwide who responded to the *Lives Lived Well* surveys, with these examples from the UK:

> Our whole curriculum is geared towards independence. So is our staffing rationale and training.
> It (Independence) is a central thread in our main school and post-16 curriculums. Our school processes, systems and policies are all constructed and refined with this aim in mind.
> Everything we do supports this – resource provision, curriculum provision human resource provision.

. . . and these, too, from respondents to the international survey in Finland, Spain and Thailand:

> The ethos of teaching is to help pmld students be as independent as possible.

We try to encourage the greatest possible autonomy in all of their developmental areas . . . we try to provide them with a present and specially with a future where they can be as independent as possible.

We will support them to do every activity that they can do.

The result of this extraordinary commitment from around the world to support these young people to be as independent is summed up by teachers in Singapore and Thailand like this:

They get a sense of joy and satisfaction when they can do things on their own without help from others.

They will feel proud and will be brave to try to do everything by themselves.

Before we look, however, in more detail at the many ways schools support young people with PMLD to be independent, it is important to say, as we have before, that there is not equality of opportunity for them around the world, a fact highlighted starkly in this comment from a country whose name we have left out:

The current infrastructure (i.e. buildings, roads, public transport, health care) is not yet ready to support independence in my opinion and unless that infrastructure is improved, a lot of people with pmld will not be able to live independent lives.

Developing and expressing independence

To turn to the ways schools work to "create opportunities for these young people to do things independently", the key is yet again, and as with wellbeing, discussed in Chapter 6, "the time you invest in getting to know your pupils", with the words of a teaching assistant from Hungary echoing many of the responses: "I try to get to know each child that much that I can understand their nonverbal communication form(s)."

Central also is identifying what many schools call the learner's 'motivators' or more commonly their likes and dislikes so that personalised provision can be planned based around those motivators to support independence as much as possible. Just one example of this, provided by a school in the UK, describes a pupil who only really likes soft textures, so as far as is possible, the activities planned for this young person are based around soft textures because this "will only increase his independence" as these are the things he has chosen for himself. Our teaching assistant (TA) at the Steiner School in Hungary also goes on to explain that once she has spent that important time getting to know her pupil's nonverbal communication, "if he or she really wants to do something but it cannot happen at that moment, I make sure that the child knows that as he or she made his or her wish clear, it will be honoured later".

Pedagogically, this approach is summarised by another school as "learning which follows the pupil's intent" underpinned by a pedagogical process we usually call scaffolding and a "gradual reduction of support" to increase independent activity, with the key worker from Kenya explaining that "support is provided only when they have tried a task and cannot independently do it" and another key worker, this time from Thailand, reiterating that "they should be assisted in the beginning of practice, then the assistances should be gradually decreased to encourage them to be more independent".

Many of the respondents from the international survey discuss the importance of transferable skills or what a teacher trainer from Taiwan calls "making classroom learning as functional as possible" so that, in the words of an Israeli teacher, teaching can "connect to their world", because this will ensure they "learn more and advance towards independence". A Spanish teacher also stresses the importance of working in "real situations" or, at the very least, "designing activities they can generalise later", with a Thai researcher favouring finding "opportunities to apply those learned skills to real-life". We look a bit more closely at this later on in this chapter when we discuss 'life skills'.

Schools acknowledge that independence can be expressed in many ways but also fully agree with a classroom assistant from Singapore that we must also "allow them to make mistakes". Some schools entrust their pupils with key 'jobs' around the school, such as, from the UK, "taking the register to the office, or taking the dinner list" and, in a classroom in Israel, "one student brings back the lunch trolley after meals, and other students help the teacher water the plants by accompanying her outside and pressing a button to turn on the water".

More usually, however, and especially remembering the definitions of PMLD discussed in Chapter 1, independence is expressed with "small steps each day," and one key issue discussed right across the surveys is that as well as diverse opportunities to experience independence, these young people must be "given [a] length of time to respond", with teachers in Spain describing this process as "time to answer, and time to listen," and going on to say that patience is required on the part of the staff around the child so that "help is only given if they need it". The teacher, as one goes on to emphasise "must not anticipate the answer", and from a teacher in Israel, we hear that "the teachers and staff wait for reactions before continuing with each activity, to make sure that they don't miss anything".

Expressions of independence can be encouraged simply by asking something like "Which sock would you like me to take off first?" and then all independent engagement – even what one describes as "a wiggle" – is acknowledged and honoured as an expression of choice and autonomy. The following wonderful example of the subtle minutiae of independence for these young people also highlights the rewards of working with this group which we have all felt so many times:

> For one pupil independence could simply be moving their fingers, and this would be celebrated.

In fact, it is quite wonderful and heartening how many times in the questionnaires words like *honoured*, *celebrated* and *respected* are used by schools when describing their response to their pupils with PMLD. This makes us feel that young people with PMLD are certainly in the right hands!

Choice?

We have seen in the discussion of literature and policy in Part I that 'choice' is usually seen as one of the key indicators of independence (Johnson & Walmsley, 2010) in all of us, and schools that responded to the surveys clearly endorse this with many, many references over the more than 100 responses to the learners being giving opportunities for 'choice', 'to choose' or perhaps, more important, "to make better choices" when schools describe how they encourage these young people to be independent. Examples of this are given as "choosing between a series of photos in order to choose what activity they want", "yes/no answers about what they want to do/eat/wear etc", "choices of toys, or songs", "choices as to what they would like to do in leisure time, choices for materials and access to staff during lessons" and "choices over the day, for eating, art activities and play time". A psychologist in Spain also stresses the importance of learners having "a chosen space with their peers where they can feel among equals", and a lead teacher in the US underlines the importance not only of offering real choices to the young person herself but also of "teaching our parents and related service providers (e.g. physiotherapists, speech therapists and occupational therapists) to offer choices, and to use wait time". Patience, it is becoming clear, is one of the key skills or a successful practitioner in this field.

In many cases, what one Spanish teacher calls "compensatory means" are used to help pupils express choice with 'switch' devices as well as "buddy buttons and touch technology" and Picture Exchange Systems (PECS) used widely by learners to express preferences or in other ways to influence the environment around them, such as to "control a range of equipment and resources" and "control the environment using switches" or simply "using switches to turn things on and off", although one teacher in Israel cautions against an overreliance on these sorts of devices by constantly "revaluating the student's abilities and weaknesses and matching the correct aids to their current abilities. This ensures that the aids don't stunt the students' progress, but rather helps them move forward".

'Choice', however, as we have seen, is not always offered in ways which empower the young person especially if we cannot be sure the young person fully understands the choices available or when simple binary choices are offered in the form of 'yes/no' cards or laminated symbols, and this is reflected by a teacher in Australia who has found that sometimes "behaviourist approaches can be a bit dehumanising (even with the best of intentions)".

We discuss a little later in this chapter how schools do work to access the true and authentic 'voices' of these young people, but sadly, it is important to acknowledge as we have before in this book that in some places and for a number of reasons, schools may not be able to offer regular and real choices to the young person, as in these responses to the international survey:

> As much as we try to give them choices, it is usually the staff who choose what activity they do, what time they eat etc.
> Rarely will people with pmld be given opportunities to express choices because they will be in schools with limited funding, and neither are they supported by social services to ensure their choices or opinions matter. Basically, it is more of 'be grateful for the services you get' rather than what they would like to do.
> In the global picture many people with pmld do not have a way to express choices and opinions for themselves.

Echoing to a certain extent these and other concerns in the literature (Vorhaus, 2015) about how 'choice' is framed and defined when applied to the group, a significant number of respondents preferred the terms 'control', 'impact' or 'affect' as summarised by "every effort is made to ensure that pupils realise the [e]ffect that they can have upon their world and the people in it", simply because, and who would disagree, "control over your own life is so important!" Giving a clear indication that simply expressing a binary choice between two objects or activities is not enough, a Spanish physiotherapist insists that "a holistic approach highlights empowerment" and that these young people, like us all, "want to feel empowered". This word, *empowerment*, comes up a lot in the international surveys around the world, with a researcher in Norway explaining that 'empowerment' itself is at the heart of policy in his country:

> There is a tremendous focus on securing individual rights in Norway. These days, participation (*medvirkning*) is also at the forefront. The term in Norwegian is close[ly] linked to influence or perhaps empowerment. I think this seems to be the main focus, as well as involving families and friends, and ensuring plenty of opportunities to be active and participate in the community.

In general, the respondents to the *Lives Lived Well* surveys echo the findings of the literature and, in particular, Woolf (2010), who reminds us that without conventional or clear pathways for expressing choice and autonomy, the lives of people with PMLD run the risk of becoming nothing more than an "epiphenomenon of other people's decisions" (p. 153), with a key worker in Thailand telling us that "the voices of those individuals are made by their parents rather than themselves" and a speech and language therapist from Singapore acknowledging that "it can be challenging for the staff to embed the communication opportunities the students need". The Norwegian researcher who we have heard from before picks up on this point by commenting that in his country, although "there is a huge focus on individual assistants," the reality is that this "has both advantages and disadvantages". This apparent abundance of personal assistants in one wealthier country is not experienced everywhere, however, and from one teacher in Europe, for instance, we hear this: "if he needs an assistant to help him be independent, in our country it is a big problem".

Physical independence

Setting aside this discussion of the advantages, disadvantages and availability of personal assistants, one American lead teacher stresses the importance of "doing things *with* our students rather than *for* them to help promote independence". This is particularly relevant to issues around postural management, and the question of whether being the receiver of physical routines and being 'done to' can compromise a person's dignity and independence. The MOVE programme (www. enhamtrust.org.uk/move) is cited by more than one UK respondent as helping to "ensure maximum independence in functional mobility", and another school in the UK places a "heavy focus on independent movement and interpretation" with a teacher in Israel describing her work with preschool-age children as "focusing on motor independence, in whatever way possible. For some, this may be better head control, and for others, it can be scooting, crawling, or walking with a walker". Others take a more general approach with "provision of free time – unguided sessions with a simple stimulus which enable pupils to engage without adult intervention" or simply "allowing 'free time' out of chairs", an approach summed up succinctly, and again rather inspiringly, as follows:

If pupils want to stand up, move, go for a walk this is respected and honoured.

Here again, technology, such as powered wheelchairs and devices to support walking which we discussed more fully in Chapter 6, are cited as enabling independent movement, simply because, as one respondent puts it, "he is able to control it". Some countries, of course, have more money for technologies such as these than others with one researcher commenting: "Norway is a wealthy country and can therefore spend a lot more on technologies to assist people in becoming more mobile, communicating easier, etc.". Sadly, however, this is not the case everywhere. A few schools in the UK mention the design of their school building as being specifically geared towards fostering independence, however, without giving any real detail about what that might entail though one does describe a new building "purpose built with PMLD pupils at the heart of the design".

Independence in personal care

Moving on from school design, as any teacher of young people with PMLD will know, 'domestic and personal care' is a central part of the school day for these young people and the adults who work with them. It is also a very broad field, with a Spanish teacher explaining that in her school "bathroom/hygiene routines are probably the most emphasised" whilst others cite routines around feeding and dressing, and we look at all these and more in greater detail when we discuss 'life skills' a little later in this chapter. All these routines, however, run the risk of compromising both independence and dignity for a young person, and this is specifically acknowledged by one of the UK residential schools whose policy is that "staff are trained to support in the least intrusive or disruptive way".

Approaches to preserve as much independence as possible during personal care described by the respondents range from "being verbally encouraged to join in where possible, with tasks such as brushing teeth and washing hands etc." to pupils being "assisted in contributing to personal care routines", a process outlined in more detail as follows:

Students are encouraged to use any movement they do have to support with their personal care e.g. lifting their hips up, rolling with a prompt, indicating which way they want to roll.

84 Part II

Of course, as with any young person, independence does not always mean compliance, and it is always important to recognise that a young person with PMLD just like everybody else has the right to say no. One of the participants in the online focus group recalls pupils he has taught who are very capable indeed of exercising their independent right not to cooperate:

> I have taught several students who close their eyes and pretend to be asleep in order to avoid an activity with someone they don't know or like, and others I have worked with throw an arm or both of their arms out to the side just before they are about to go through a door-way when manoeuvred by an adult.

And I think we all know what that feels like!

There is an important point here which was touched on in Part I and that is that there are discrepancies between conventional definitions of independence and the actual lives of people with PMLD, but this doesn't mean that independence on their own terms has to be elusive for these young people. One of the respondents emphasises the importance of acknowledging the "atypical ways our PMLD pupils display independence", with one of the contributors to the online focus group agreeing that "pupils with PMLD sometimes find their own very unique ways of exercising control over their environment". It is, of course, a question of trust – trusting the young person enough to allow them to explore their own boundaries of independence – and here is a marvellous example of this again from our TA at that Steiner School in Hungary who describes a child who "always runs away and wants to climb up a small hill during a walking trip. I let her do this, tell her that she needs to come back, and trust that she will do it by herself. . . . Most of the time she does".

Life skills

On a more pragmatic level, several respondents mention 'life skills' as being central to the independence of this cohort with "lots of opportunities across the day to practice life skills", the setting of "specific life skills targets within Educational Health and Care (EHC) Plans" and the use of "Pre-Entry level qualifications that focus on developing life skills at a level appropriate for each learner". One of the schools with residential provision also benefits from "a fully adapted flat where they can be assessed and practice using assistive technology which can then be installed in their own home where appropriate".

In both the UK online focus group and in the international survey, participants were asked to list what they thought the essential life skills were for young people with PMLD to be as independent as possible, and this produced, not surprisingly, a rich and eclectic list, with 'choice' or 'informed choices', which we have already looked at in this chapter, being popular, however not nearly as popular as communication with several respondents choosing to emphasis this with capital letters ("COMMUNICATION"), exclamation marks ("Communication!!!") or even both ('COMMUNICATION!!!'). So, to do these enthusiastic responses justice, we discuss 'communication' as a life skill in a bit more detail later when we look at 'voice'. But to return to those lists of life skills, whilst agreeing with one Spanish teacher that, of course, "we are all different", we can very broadly divide the suggestions into what we might for convenience call 'hard' and 'soft' life skills.

The useful 'hard' skills suggested by respondents to the *Lives Lived Well* surveys focus mostly on what many call "self-help" or "self-care", including washing, bathing, toileting, toothbrushing and dressing. Skills around eating and drinking are also commonly put forward as being essential, with several suggesting "holding the spoon", another prioritising "small improvements in chewing and swallowing food" and one going so far as to suggest "being able to prepare simple recipes such as tea, toast, or a sandwich". We fully acknowledge that preparing food may be challenging for many young people with PMLD, but it is our experience as teachers that simple drinks, tea or a snack as suggested here may be a realistic aim for some. Many other suggestions focus broadly on mobility and especially "autonomy of movement", with, in some cases, the use of "assistive technology" such as "walking alone on the walker towards an object", while for others this is framed more in terms of community access such as "going shopping", "using public transport" and again, ambitiously but not necessarily unrealistically, "exchanging money with the cashier in a shop".

Almost inevitably, the types of 'soft' skills put forward as essential for this group are harder to define but no less meaningful, so we present some of the most common of them in a simple alphabetical list as each

86 Part II

will have significance in different ways for each young person with PMLD in the world:

- Empowerment

- Engagement

- Perseverance

- Problem-solving

- Resilience

- Responsiveness

- Self-acceptance

- Self-advocacy

- Self-awareness

- Self-determination

Some responses echo our discussions in Chapter 6 about the importance of "impacting directly on their immediate environment" as well as on "social participation", "social skills" and "the ability to build relationships", whilst others place an emphasis on skills which we know are vital to the wellbeing of us all but are possibly less acknowledged as such for young people with PMLD, skills defined by a Spanish physiotherapist as "emotional freedom" and described by others as "coping with stress"; "recognising how they feel, and why, and how to communicate this"; or, simply, in the words of a social worker from Spain, "what is needed at a personal level to be happy". A few, however, make the important point that no matter how many life skills are required, there are probably none more important than "the ability to recognize a danger or abuse situation" and "being able to ask for help", and one respondent refrains from listing life skills but puts forward one thing which should always come first: "people with PMLD and their families need to be listened to." All these points and more are picked up and illustrated in Part III when we look at practice at Chailey Heritage School in Sussex.

Independent sexual beings

We have seen already in Part I of this book that there is a concern that a key indicator of independence for all young people "the right to express themselves as sexual beings" (Jordan, 2013) can be problematic for those with PMLD. To explore this in the *Lives Lived Well* UK survey, respondents were asked how they felt young people could be supported in this area, and this was one of the few questions which asked for a personal opinion. This was the least answered of the questions in the UK survey possibly because of the potentially complex ethical and cultural issues around this issue, and this was, in fact, a reason why it was decided – rightly or wrongly – to leave this question out of the international survey.

Many of those UK teachers and school leaders who did respond acknowledged their own difficulties in addressing issues of sexuality for this group, with responses including "no idea", "no view", "I don't know", "this is a tricky area", and "I need training or support", although one respondent does suggest a reason for at least some of these difficulties:

> I am sad to say that this is not possible in the current system which is totally geared towards protection and infantilising these people. It would need parent agreement and very brave therapists.

Clearly, however, it is an issue which many practitioners feel needs to be addressed and some schools are beginning to move forward, although this is often expressed as an intention rather than as school policy and with reference to the whole school across a range of needs rather than looking at specific issues with those with PMLD:

> We are currently reviewing our relationships and sexuality policies and provision.
> Through personal, social, health and economic (PSHE) and sex and relationship education (SRE) lessons.
> Through specific training for students with SEN [special educational needs].
> All the pupils received appropriate PSHE lessons.

With specific reference to young people with PMLD, effective support in this area is described as "person specific" and on a "case by case basis" because "sexuality needs to freely develop but be developmentally supported", and there is a suggestion that "good counsellors would help along with staff that know them well and excellent open relationships with carers and parents". The development of good communication skills is also seen as essential so that "the learner would be able to express their sexuality, needs and desires".

There is an acknowledgement also that these young people "often struggle with what is appropriate within their sexual development", and perhaps because of this, there are several references to the importance of ensuring the dignity and safety of each individual as well as the provision of safe or private spaces and "the right to say no".

There is very little detail though around actual provision or support which could be used to allow young people with PMLD to express themselves as sexual beings, and just three UK respondents describe strategies to enable independent sexual expression for young people in this group, although in all three cases, it is unclear whether these are enacted as part of school practice or simply suggestions, and of course, they will be controversial for some readers, both parents and practitioners:

> Being given time to explore their body in a safe space.
> Time at home without pads on.
> If a student shows a particular interest in another peer, e.g. by reaching out to them, then this is encouraged and facilitated, drawing both students' attention to the interaction.

Despite the difficulties and sensitivities addressing issues of sexual expression for young people with PMLD, one respondent points at least towards the future in this area of provision: "we should not shy away from it".

Voice?

We discussed earlier how 'choice' is a key indicator of independence for all of us and none more so than those with PMLD. We have also seen, however, that what 'choice' means is sometimes complex for this

Lives Lived Well surveys: independence **89**

group and that expressing it authentically can be compromised by a number of factors. We have also seen here and in Chapter 6 that 'communication' in all its forms is always seen as central to expressions of independence for this group, and many of the suggestions for appropriate life skills to support independence are related to communication, such as refusing, requesting, attracting attention, drawing others into engagements, having social interactions with familiar and unfamiliar people and "developing a consistent yes/no response".

Yet, as all parents, teachers and other practitioners know all too well, these tend to be aims or targets, and actual opportunities for the voice, opinion and feelings of someone with PMLD to be heard in the here and now can be compromised by aspects of their condition, a factor acknowledged by a teacher in Israel as "very challenging as the students often can't move on their own and do not search out their peers". Possibly more important, affirming the independent 'voice' of a young person with PMLD can be problematic for us, the listener, when that 'voice' is expressed in what more than one school calls "atypical ways". So a key focus of the *Lives Lived Well* surveys was to explore from a school's point of view how we affirm and listen to the true 'voice' of the young person, and this may help us answer Johnson and Walmsley's (2010) simple but unavoidable question: "How do we find out what people with disabilities want?"

For many schools, accessing a pupil's voice "in whatever form that takes", as one of them puts it, is part of their core ethos alongside approaches to wellbeing and independence:

> The whole school experience is built around the child to ensure their voice is heard among all the other voices in their family.
> All learning is intertwined to support communication.
> Ensuring our pupils have the communication tools they need is the best way of ensuring pupil voice for this group.
> This aspect is very important in our school. We always think about the student's voice. We try to give them the tools to express themselves. The goal is to help every student to have a clear as possible 'yes' and 'no' until they leave school.
> I think this is something we excel at in our school. Every person has a voice and an opinion. By teaching our students that their message is important and heard is critical.

In the UK, schools are ensuring that targets around communication are firmly embedded in EHC Plans as part of what one respondent describes as an "inclusive Annual Review process", with the young people, as well as their advocates, attending planning meetings "to ensure the learner's voice is not lost", and in other parts of the world too, as here in Israel, "most of the yearly goals for each student revolve around advancing communication abilities so that their voice is heard".

As with so much of the good practice from around the world described in this book, classroom approaches to liberating each young person's voice are primarily "personalised and based around pupil motivators", and in some schools, "the students decide what lesson they would like to do based on their preferences on that day" or use "communication symbols to indicate whether they want to participate in a specific activity".

Many schools use "communication passports", "important to me bags" or "listen to me documents" which give a picture of the learner's likes and dislikes, motivators, interests and "individual communication strategies", with these resources in the Steiner School in Hungary being referred to evocatively as "a book of their lives" and including information such as "where they live, who they live with, pets, siblings, weekend activities, relatives". In these ways, learning can be adapted if students show a particular interest in an experience: "We always build on those things that create a positive response" and "acknowledging their responses wherever possible", with several schools again emphasising that key message that pupils also have "the right to say no".

Observation, patience, "utilizing pause or wait time", "careful interpretation of body language", interpreting behaviour in all its forms and simply "spending quality time with the pupils" are cited as the starting points for valid and meaningful communication as an expression of independence, expressed by a teacher in Israel as follows:

We work according to their facial expressions, sounds and body language. We always look at them, reflect their actions and give words and feeling to those reactions.

Opportunities are maximised for pupils to communicate through their "preferred methods", with adult support as needed and what is again called "honouring" of all efforts at communication by "adults who read their cues/communications and respond accordingly", searching, as one Israeli teacher puts it, for even "the slightest response to stimulus" when these cues can simply be "a little flutter of a finger or blinking their eyes", "an eye twitch or slight hand movement" or, what one respondent calls almost poetically, "a stilling". If anything encapsulates this notion of total communication" which is mentioned in so many schools, it is surely this. After all, I use my voice every day, all day, sometimes I use it too much, but for someone with PMLD, a simple stillness, a pause, can express as much as I can in all those words.

Listening in all its many forms is also key to accessing the voice of the young person, and this is something which comes across particularly in the international surveys. A student teacher in Israel talks strongly of her "yearning to hear the persons wants and needs even if it is difficult to understand", a teacher in Spain talks of "listening to their body language", and a physiotherapist in the same country talks of her pupils "insisting on being heard". Perhaps it is not surprising then, as we have seen in Chapter 6, that intensive interaction (Hewett, 2018) is widely used "to develop the fundamentals of communication", as well as "body signing", which as many readers will know is a way of using touch cues to build a 'vocabulary' and communicate with the child with very complex needs.

Speech therapy, of course, is widely offered in many – although not all – countries and a large number of alternative and augmentative communication (AAC) strategies and resources are used, with a teacher in Massachusetts listing "objects of reference, pictures, partial objects, sign language, eye-gaze, speech, print, braille, augmentative communication, devices-high and low tech". At the high-tech end, we hear quite extensively of eye-gaze technology, iPads, talking mats, switches, voice output communication aids (VOCAS) and other less well-known technologies such as pragmatic organisation dynamic display (PODD; www.inclusive.co.uk/podd-p6023), which is an organisational communication assessment scheme, although, again, the ability to offer these often expensive communication supports to young people can be compromised in some countries, with one teacher lamenting that "given the poor economy, eye-tracking devices and switches do not exist in schools".

Not everyone relies on high tech, however, to engage their learners and encourage independence. In one school in Singapore, for instance, learners with PMLD are "given platforms to shine", by "letting their voices be heard in various carnivals and events in which they can participate", and at a school in the UK, pupils with PMLD are encouraged to "explore the sound of Shakespeare", which may not be as far-fetched as it sounds if we remember that in *King Lear*, Shakespeare's advice "have more than you show; speak less than you know" is also a fairly neat way of defining two of the many wonderful and unique attributes of a person with PMLD.

Whose voice is it anyway?

Nevertheless, for a young person with PMLD, decision-making will often rely rightly or wrongly on the advocacy of others for the rest of their life, a fact recognised in the UK in the *Special Education Needs and Disabilities (SEND) Code of Practice* – "some young people may require support in expressing their Views" (DfE, 2015, p. 258) – and is enshrined in law in other countries such as Norway, where "regular meetings with the individual and their family/supporters is required by law". This is a fact of life neither denied nor disputed by the vast majority of the respondents to the *Lives Lived Well* surveys worldwide. "We educators are their voices", says a teacher in Singapore, echoing the sentiments of a UK teacher: "Our students depend upon other people to read their intentions and communicate these to the outside world". Who or what that proxy voice should be, however, as well as how it should be expressed and to what extent it can be considered to be the true 'voice' of the young person are much more open to debate.

Proxy voice

The *Lives Lived Well* UK and international surveys addressed this issue of the proxy voice directly. First, participants were asked to

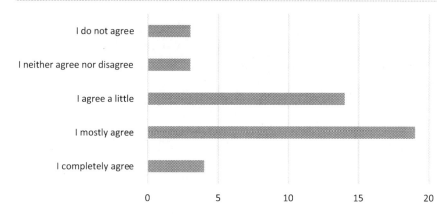

Figure 7.1 UK survey: To what extent do you agree that a 'proxy' voice such as that of a parent, carer or intervenor can be considered to represent the 'voice' or the 'opinion' of the young person.

rate on a 5-point scale from 'I do not agree' to 'I completely agree' to what extent they felt a 'proxy' voice such as that of a parent, carer or intervenor can be considered to represent the 'voice' or the 'opinion' of the young person. The UK survey produced the results shown in Figure 7.1.

The international survey produced broadly similar results, although opinions were a little more polarised from the UK, where 7% did not agree at all and 53.5% either completely or mostly agreed whereas internationally only 4.5% did not agree and only 47.5% mostly or completely agreed, as shown in Figure 7.2.

Clearly then, a majority of people working with this group of young people do see the value of a 'proxy' voice, and in a follow-up question, when the participants were asked if they had any further comments on this issue, many extol the benefits of this role:

> For many people with pmld this proxy is the only voice to express choice or opinion.
>
> (Parent, Spain)

When we are referring to students with PMLD, it is crucial having a proxy to fight for the right to have a good education, being

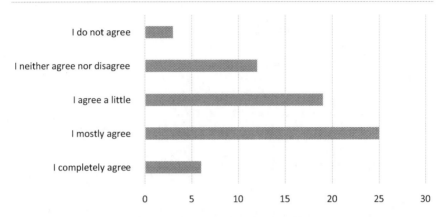

Figure 7.2 International survey: To what extent do you agree that a 'proxy' voice such as that of a parent, carer or intervenor can be considered to represent the 'voice' or 'opinion' of the young person?

assisted with dignity and to claim the support the families so desperately need as they get older.

(Speech and language therapist, Spain)

Many, however, whilst broadly in favour of the concept of a proxy, stress that this person should be trained or at least "under supervision", and some often and quite understandably have other reservations or caveats which broadly echo the words of two American teachers that "it needs to be evaluated on an individual basis" because "I still believe that teaching our students to voice for themselves is critical in whatever way is possible", and others see a proxy more or less as a last resort:

> Often there is no choice but steps should be taken first to ascertain the person's own choices.
>
> (Researcher, Israel)

> It should exist only if it is completely necessary, and perhaps have their representative functions evolving or decreasing as needed over time.
>
> (Physiotherapist, Spain)

Lives Lived Well surveys: independence **95**

Despite the quite small numbers at 7% and 4.5% across both surveys not agreeing that a proxy voice can represent the child, in the follow-up question, some strong views were expressed against proxies:

> It is an illusion to say that a 'proxy' voice represents the voice of the young person.
> There is no voice that can be a true representation of what the child wants to say.
> Every student has a voice and we need to learn their individual ways.
> A person cannot be the representative of another person.
> Proxy should not represent the targeted person.

One of the common reservations given about a proxy being a true representative of the child is the fear that this person may have their own agenda as in these responses from Australia and the UK:

> Unless the proxy is trained, their agenda is likely to be deeply influenced by the agenda/income bracket/social experience/age/experience/cultural perspective/aspirations of the proxy.
> Some 'proxy' voices have their own agenda, be it political, related to money/benefits, rather than being an advocate for the actual person involved.

However, as with those in favour of proxies, even those who expressed themselves strongly against the concept of a proxy representing the young person often were prepared to compromise or qualify their remarks as in the following from the international surveys:

> Although I do not agree with the figure of a "proxy", with some students it is very difficult to recognise their opinions as they do not communicate verbally.
>
> (Teacher, Spain)

> It is complex and problematic, and where parents have understanding and awareness it is possible, but even then this needs to be treated with caution.
>
> (Advisor to the government of Timor Leste)

At least their rights are protected and their voices are heard.

(Key worker, Thailand)

With respect to this role being carried out by parents or carers, there are significantly more international than UK respondents who think that the parents would be the best proxy for their child, as in these examples:

Parents or carers might understand the person with PMLD better than others. They are able to interpret the meaning of their gestures better, so their needs can be met in an easier way.

(Speech and language therapist, Spain)

The parents often know their child best.

(Teacher, Israel)

Parents may understand their child's habit and help people who are unfamiliar with the child to understand his communication style.

(Teacher, Singapore)

UK respondents tend to be more guarded in their support for parents as proxy voices, as in the following:

Most parents would be a very safe voice, a small minority not.
I would hope that a person whether it be parent carer or other would always hold the best interests of the young person at the forefront, however I feel that there may be occasions where this would not be the case.

And the following are from the international surveys:

Parents and carers play important roles in the lives of persons with PMLD. Based on their experiences and interactions with them, they may be able to infer what gestures or facial expressions mean but will not be able to represent their opinions fully.

(Teacher, Singapore)

It does help for the parent or the main caregiver to help interpret some of the behaviours and reactions since it is assumed that they would know after having spent a lot more time with the child. However, I think it is important for educators to also use their own experience and discretion when considering if the 'proxy' voice truly reflects the needs and voice of the young person.

(Teacher, Singapore)

It depends on the family. There are families who are really involved, and know their son/daughters well and they understand them very well, even if there is no language. But there are also families that show very little interest towards the interests of their son/daughters and only look to their own comfort and choice.

(Psychologist, Spain)

In general, then, a quite negative view of the ability of parents to represent their child as a proxy is more prevalent in the UK responses, with these extracts from the questionnaire fairly representative of the whole:

A parent may well voice their own concerns and not really listen or understand the needs of their child.

Parents present a view mostly from their perspective and not that of their young person.

We can only do our best to express what we think the young person needs. It can't be known fully.

We have to be sure that any parent/carer etc who is trying to be the voice for the young person has the best interests of the young person as priority.

This, of course, is in line with current UK guidance in the form of the *SEND Code of Practice* (2015) that "local authorities must not use the views of parents as a proxy for young people's views" (DfE, 2015, p. 22) and reflects warnings in the literature of "an over reliance on interpretation by parents and carers where the children have little verbal communication" (Watson, Abbott, & Townsley, 2006).

So what do practitioners think are the qualities required to be an effective proxy or in the words of a social worker from Spain the 'person of reference' and, if not parents, who should the proxy be?

In terms of the qualities required to be an effective proxy, wanting the best for the child and having their best interest at heart come up regularly as well as knowing the person in depth, and not just listening to them but also "representing them in their truest form" and, importantly, "respecting" them, as a teacher from Slovakia puts it. Others talk of the importance of "finding new ways of understanding them" and "making an effort to find out ways of enhancing the well-being of the person with pmld". The ability not just to be their 'voice' but to also advocate for them within what a teacher in Australia calls "a system that operates beyond their realm of understanding" is frequently discussed also though outside the UK often this is seen as the responsibility of "disability associations", specialist self-advocacy groups of "parent groups".

So who would be an appropriate independent advocate to represent the voice of a young person with PMLD bearing in mind what we have seen so far that "it is often better to have someone who is not so emotionally attached to speak for them" and that preferably "they have to have had a long standing relationship"?

A few from the UK survey suggest "the teacher rather than the parent", but most of the UK respondents hold the view that it should not be one person but "a small group who know the pupil well" because this would be the only way that "a fair and true proxy voice may be heard", and this is summed up by one teacher in Australia as "a number of voices, professional, educational, family and where possible the young person, seem to be the best way of achieving a consensual support network". Nor would these people just be drawn from those working directly with the pupil at the time but, rather, "a team so the pupil's voice in all areas, all time frames, and across their life is taken into consideration", including contributions from "environments such as respite and youth clubs to get a rounded picture of the student" or, in other words, "a range of people who know the person in different capacities to present a broad picture to prevent bias and personal interest", and in fact, in Spain, this approach is given the wonderfully evocative name *proyecto vital de la persona* or the "person's vital life project".

Again, however, we conclude another section of this book, this time on proxy voice, with reports from two very different parts of the world that financial issues mean that many young people with PMLD do not even have the chance to work with someone as their 'proxy' voice. From one we hear, "I do not see this happening in this country as the special education sector is already budgeted poorly and is not seen as a priority for government". And a key worker from a very different part of the world explains that

> sadly, the value of a proxy is not fully supported by adequate legislation within schools and colleges and therefore, they have not support mechanisms to fall on to, to fight for the rights of the people they support. In comparison to developed countries, we do not have adequate lobby groups to efficiently support or advocate the value of proxies and disability has never been placed as a top priority in national matters.

Who cares for the carers?

Finally, however, in this chapter, we want to turn our attention to the parents and carers themselves. They may not be seen by some as the best advocates or proxy voice for their child, but it is an unavoidable fact that people with PMLD will be dependent on the support of others for their whole lives and that this will almost always be their parents or carers while they are able to do so.

One of the questions in the UK questionnaire asked teachers how they ensure parents remained fully informed and involved in their child's learning and development over and above annual reviews and other essential meetings. This question was not part of the international survey because, as we have explained in Chapter 5, we were not able on an international level to target teachers specifically, but nevertheless, we hear from a teacher in Singapore that "parents are invited to be in their child's class so as to see how skills are taught. Parents can then transfer these skills when at home", and a similar approach from a school in Spain that "work[s] with families so that they can continue schoolwork at home."

The results from the UK survey show that there is an emphasis on direct contact from school through phone calls, communication books, emails and some home visits by teachers and therapists.

To facilitate these communications, social media and other digital platforms are popular and, in particular, apps which allow videos and pictures to be sent home often in real time such as *Seesaw Communication* (https://web.seesaw.me/), *Evidence for Learning* (www.evidencefor learning.net/) and *Marvellous Me* (https://marvellousme.com/).

In general, then, "close relationships with families" are the norm for this group, as is, of course, "contact with social services where these are accessed by the child", and there is a great deal of "open dialogue with parents", with schools clearly working hard to foster "excellent relationships" with them.

As we have seen in the literature, however (e.g. Nussbaum, 2007), there are wider concerns about the long-term wellbeing of parents and carers, especially where they are "stigmatised by dependency'" (Kittay, 2011, p. 51), and this concern is shared by the respondents to the *Lives Lived Well* surveys who were asked in if they thought that families with a member with PMLD live isolated and unfulfilled lives (see Figures 7.3 and 7.4).

The percentage of respondents across the UK and international surveys who either mostly or completely agreed was similar, at 47% and 45%, respectively, while the proportion of those who did not agree was perhaps worryingly small in both surveys at 8% and 9%, respectively, with more than one of the international respondents putting forward one of the reasons why that might be:

> Family members need to work to make ends meet, hence have no or little time to spend with their children.
>
> (Teacher, Singapore)

On top of everything they already do, schools that teach young people with PMLD then perhaps have even more work to do to support isolated and unfulfilled parents and carers on top of their statutory duties to teach their pupils.

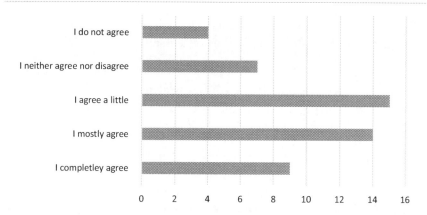

Figure 7.3 UK survey: Do you agree that families with a disabled member live isolated and unfulfilled lives?

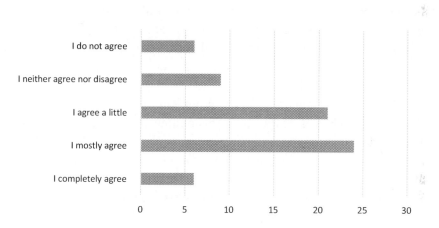

Figure 7.4 International survey: Do you agree that families with a disabled member live isolated and unfulfilled lives?

The schools that answered the *Lives Lived Well* survey do this by giving advice, running workshops, parent support groups, what one respondent in India describes as "parent training involving community partners" and, from Spain, "comfort circles for them and their families". The focus around the world is clearly on asking families what support they want and doing their best to provide that. In short, whenever they can they "support parents with carers' fatigue", as one UK

102 Part II

teacher describes it, and a teacher in Spain gives a bit more detail of the essential work they do with families in her school:

> We focus on listening to what families tell us, and provide them with what they are interested in as well as workshops to cope with their worries, and emotional wellbeing, to avoid them feeling lonely or feeling singled out.

In the UK at least, formalising this support for the wider family through Education, Health and Care (EHC) Plans is, however, more problematic, with only two UK schools acknowledging that they try to ensure the needs of parents and carers are addressed in section E of the document, with one citing an actual outcome as "to be able to call for help via a switch at home" and another that an outcome for the whole family might simply be "to remain healthy and well". Partly this may be because, as one respondent puts it, "the local authority won't allow it!" with another explaining, "This is something that we would love to do but isn't supported by the local authority. Outcomes must relate to the young person". So there is an ambiguity here at the heart of UK policy. Young people with PMLD will be dependent on parents and carers for their whole lives; this interdependency is inevitable, and yet the associated needs of those parents and carers cannot be accounted for in planning.

Other outcomes set in EHC Plans can be said to have a less direct impact on the wellbeing of parents and carers, such as those which support the independence of the young person within the home environment with for example "a ramp at home to support independence" and the following extracts from actual EHC Plans which school generously and anonymously shared with us:

> He will have self-help skills at a level so that he can consistently wash his hands with minimal adult support and be more independent in eating on his own.
>
> He will be able to stand up for five minutes holding onto a supportive rail, so that his pad can be changed in a disabled toilet. This kind of outcome will mean that the family are able to include (name) in a wider variety of community activities.

Occasionally, it is the provision of respite care as an outcome in an EHC Plan which respondents cite as having the most significant impact on the wellbeing of the rest of the family:

> For the student to have regular access to residential trips, once a month, so that family have opportunities to rest, reconnect and reflect.
> Increased respite so that they can spend more time with family.

We have seen then in this chapter the number of ways large and small schools around the world work to enhance the independence of their pupils with PMLD and the expression of that independence practically, pedagogically and emotionally, and this is often achieved in the face of very real financial, systemic and cultural barriers. What 'independence' means for each individual person with PMLD is, of course, unique and, in a sense, defies definition, and one of the UK teachers who completed the *Lives Lived Well* survey suggests that for this group, at least, accepted definitions of independence and dependency may have to be revisited:

> I question accepted notions of independence as I think it seems too far off what we are really trying to achieve for pupils with pmld. Perhaps it is more a case of supporting them to be interdependent.

Perhaps then, as we begin to make links between the different chapters and themes in this book, we are finding that words like *self-fulfilment*, *belonging*, *empowerment* and *interdependence* can legitimately replace *wellbeing, community participation, choice* and *independence* when we address the very unique needs of this group of young people. By doing this, perhaps we will then truly think about them in ways which are relevant to their lives as they actually live and experience them.

In the next chapter, we look at whether it is possible for these young people to maintain their own unique levels and forms of independence once they have left school at whatever age that is around the world.

Reference list

DfE. (2015). *Special educational needs and disability code of practice: 0–25 years.* London: HMSO.

Hewett, D. (2018). *The intensive interaction handbook* (2nd ed.). London: Sage.

Johnson, K., & Walmsley, J. (2010). *People with intellectual disabilities. Towards a good life?* Bristol: The Policy Press.

Jordan, R. (2013). *Autism with severe learning difficulties* (2nd ed.). London: Souvenir Press.

Kittay, E. (2011). The ethics of care, dependence and disability. *Ratio Juris, 24*(1), 49–58.

Nussbaum, M. C. (2007). *Frontiers of justice – Disability, nationality, species membership.* Cambridge, MA: Harvard University Press.

Vorhaus, J. (2015). *Giving voice to profound disability.* London: Routledge.

Watson, D., Abbott, D., & Townsley, R. (2006). Listen to me, too! Lessons from involving children with complex healthcare needs in research about multi-agency services. *Child: Care, Health and Development, 33*(1), 90–95.

Woolf, J. (2010). Cognitive disability in a society of equals. In E. Kittay & L. Carlson (Eds.), *Cognitive disability and its challenge for moral philosophy* (pp. 147–159). Chichester: Wiley-Blackwell.

The *Lives Lived Well* surveys
Wellbeing and independence beyond school

In a departure from the structure we adopted in Chapters 6 and 7, where responses from the international survey are integrated into a general discussion around wellbeing and independence, in this and the next chapter, we start by discussing the UK context, and then we summarise the responses from the international surveys separately. We do this simply because this chapter is about provision beyond school and the next is about policy, and for the very practical reasons of time and language we were unable to make a detailed factual analysis of provision beyond school and policy in each of the 19 countries represented in the survey in the same way we are able to in the UK, a setting we were, of course, already very familiar with. The opinions expressed in the second half of this chapter then about national provision beyond school are just that: personal opinions from a range of people who work with young people in their country with profound and multiple learning difficulties (PMLD) and need to be treated as such, and as elsewhere in this book, we do at times redact the name of the country the respondent represents.

The UK context

As we have seen in the previous chapter, what is absolutely clear from the many responses to the *Lives Lived Well* surveys is that all around the world, skilled and sensitive teachers, paraprofessionals and other practitioners are working extremely hard to ensure the wellbeing of learners with PMLD, and as we said in the introduction to this book, teaching young people with the highest level of need is not only hugely rewarding but also complex and challenging.

Arguably, however, as we will see, and particularly in the UK, problems start when the young person reaches the end their compulsory schooling. Although in theory, as one school puts it, "in some ways our young people will have more opportunities to be independent because they will have developed skills towards this", it is clear from responses not only in the UK but also, as we see later, around the world that what one terms the "decline in facilities" means that in reality, they may not get the same opportunities to do things independently that they did while they were at school.

First, however, it is important to underline that schools work tirelessly to prepare their pupils – and their parents and carers – for the often difficult moment of leaving school. Whatever the school leaving age for the young person, as one respondent to the UK survey put it: "It's all in the handover", and the schools who responded to the *Lives Lived Well* survey invest time and resources in "robust transition planning" and "planning for future placement" to ensure that the young people they have been working for, in some cases, years achieve "the best transition possible". In the UK, the *Special Educational Needs and Disabilities (SEND) Code of Practice* (2015) requires schools to begin transition planning from Year 9 (age 14) and timescales mentioned by the respondents certainly reflect at least that. Long-term planning usually involves "parents exploring and trying post 19 placements as much as is possible", "taster days with possible providers" and "ensuring that the parents are aware of and exposed to as many provisions for their child". In some schools, this process is supported by a dedicated "Transition Officer", although few benefit from the level of provision described in one of the UK residential schools:

> We have an adult residential and day service provision with access to the same clinical team. We have therefore removed the 'cliff edge' associated with reaching adulthood.

Once an appropriate setting is identified, there is then most commonly an intensifying of activity "during the summer term of their last year", with a large number of the respondents emphasising the importance of sharing as much information as possible, most commonly through some kind of communication passport or pen portrait but also, in one instance from the UK, a "video transition package" sent to the new setting and increasingly the 'wiki' personal websites developed by Rix Research and Media (www.rixresearchandmedia.org) at the University of East London. Schools try to make these transition packages in whatever form they take as rigorous and informative as possible "socially, emotionally, physically and academically", including the young person's "method of interaction, their likes and dislikes, their favourite activities . . . feeding guidelines and bathroom routines" and "any assistive technology they use" and include "working with other services for transitions to adulthood such as the UK based charity Sense, college and social care". Often information to support transition is expressed in the first person, such as "how to support my social and emotional wellbeing", with one school giving a detailed first-person account of the ways one particular young person can express their independence: "I'll get cross if you don't let me have a choice so please ask me instead of choosing for me, or give me a few moments to make up my mind".

There is also evidence of the work schools in the UK do to "engage parents in decision-making" up to and including the transition to a new setting "to ensure that pupils and their families get the best possible support". One UK-based respondent summarises this as follows:

Meetings with parents are a strength – we have a clear structure of leading families through the process of transition:

- Year. 1: Mulling it over
- Year 2: Visiting the future placement and developing a Wishlist.
- Year 3: Facilitating the links and visits in an individual way.

A lot of the support offered to parents to navigate the difficult process of transition is practical and targeted, from "transition evenings" to "supporting the family to complete the forms" and even as far as "chasing funding", but schools are also all too aware of the emotional strain on parents of the prospect of their child moving to an unfamiliar setting. "We break down boundaries with parents", reports one, while for another, "We listen to the hopes of the parents and guardians", and at one of the UK residential schools which responded to the survey, "Our family services provide two link workers that support families through the college admission process".

This period of preparation is supported in many instances by transition visits by the young people with staff support and often also by staff on their own "to visualise the young adult in the potential environment". Student visits take place in some cases weekly and in others are simply described as "multiple transition visits with pupil and with families", and for many of the young people, this is a phased process so that towards the final stages of transition planning, "familiar school staff are replaced by the adult provision staff". Nor is this a one-way process. One school "invites the new support workers in to meet the pupils in our school setting and share and model activity that would be suitable", and in another, "local provisions are invited to attend training to support their staff which will help our pupils when they leave". This process is even more rigorous in residential settings where there is more time and more factors to take into account with respect to future living arrangements:

> Workers from group homes or college have liaised and stayed overnight on the premises to get a full hand-over of their needs and independence for the full 24-hour period.

The rationale behind this transition activity is, of course, not only "giving them a chance to become more familiar with the new environment" and making sure "our pupils are going on to the right place" but also having worked so hard for years with each pupil, schools want to be sure not only that skills gained in school are maintained but also that their pupils have appropriate skills for the new setting:

> We look at what skills they need to learn to be as independent as possible once they leave school: working on interaction with unfamiliar people, use of switches, standing transfers etc.
>
> Activities which promote the maintenance of existing skills or acquisition of new ones.
>
> We equip youngsters with the knowledge and skills to use their adaptive technology and devices outside of our setting and train new staff as appropriate to ensure that interventions continue in their new setting.

Lives Lived Well surveys: beyond school **109**

So there is no doubting the efforts made by schools, parents and, of course, the young people themselves to prepare for a successful transition to a new placement or provision once they leave school, and yet in the UK, at least, there is clearly a real issue in some regions with the availability of appropriate post-school provision, summed up by UK schools in these often quite bleak terms:

> Post-19 provision fails to follow up the EHC [Education, Health and Care] Plan.
> Sketchy provision beyond 19, depending where you live.
> We cannot fight for what is not available.
> There are not a great deal of options available for many students.
> What is available is often limited.

This was the problem addressed more than any other in the online focus group which followed the *Lives Lived Well* survey, with participants going into more detail about problems in their local area or region.

> The nearest provision for those with PMLD is about forty minutes' drive away . . . or out of county . . . and families have to be really proactive and push to get access to this.
> In my area there is only one official post 19 education provision . . . its old building is in a poor state of repair and has only limited specialist facilities. Lack of appropriately trained staff is also an issue.
> There are no educational provisions for post-19 people with pmld in my area . . . In seven years at my current school, I have known of two students go on to college, and both placements failed.
> We don't have a specific post 19 PMLD provision.
> There is still very little in the way of appropriate provision for those with PMLD, in particular those assessed as requiring continuing health care.

When a young person does move to a provision in a college or elsewhere some schools try to follow up or track their former pupils' progress for as long as possible, although 2 years is the longest any one school carries this on for. The work is often undertaken by the schools' Transition Officer or occasionally a link worker from the college and there is some evidence of "good working relationships with our post 19 providers with follow up support and meetings", with another emphasising "follow up work with the new provider to ensure they are maintaining students['] routines". A lot of the follow-up work, however, is more informal and short term such as "inviting students to the following year's prom" or simply trying to stay in contact with parents:

> We encourage parents to stay in touch, invite them back to whole school events.
> We call parents to check how things are going mid-September after leaving.

There is a real concern, however, that schools receive "very limited information once pupils leave the school" that "contact is significantly reduced regarding what happens to an individual's independence" and that the young people may struggle "to maintain skills they already have". Issues tracking this cohort once they have left education are described by one focus group participant as linked to data protection:

> The local authority holds destination data, and we are pushing to get access to this. However, we anticipate this will be in anonymised form due to General Data Protection Regulations (GDPR) and this will make it difficult to see where students with different types of need tend to go.

Although not a particular focus of the *Lives Lived Well* surveys, some schools in the UK lament the lack of appropriate provision for people with PMLD beyond the age of about 25. This is when "most, if not all", leave "the college provision and move to an adult social care provision". Whilst one respondent describes their nearest day-care provider as "a wonderful, multi-sensory, engaging place to be", they immediately qualify that the observation that "with the funding it receives, it is difficult to offer much in terms of education and is aimed mostly at keeping clients safe", and another respondent remarks that most of the other people in the day-care centre are "in their 50s and 60s".

For teachers around the UK then, the very real concern over what happens to their pupils is often expressed in emotive terms:

> We have very little influence over this other than showing the colleges what they can do when they leave us.
> We do not have any influence over what happens to our pupils once they have left school.
> Sadly, there is very little we do to ensure pupils continue to be comfortable, healthy and happy when they have left school age 19.
> Is there anything we could have done better?

One respondent in particular expressed the personal view that "it is my belief that our students will never have such enriched lives again after leaving us".

International contexts

As we have already touched on in Chapter 5, school provision for young people with PMLD varies considerably around the world, and this is arguably even more marked once they leave school. Very generally, and like in the UK, young adults with PMLD tend to leave compulsory schooling at between 18 and 21 years old in most countries around the world represented in the survey, and this is certainly the age reported in, among others, Australia, Cyprus, Ireland, Israel, Macedonia, Norway, Singapore, Spain and most states in the US. Lower school-leaving ages for this cohort are reported in Finland (16 years old), and India (15 years old), and our respondent in Kenya reports that "there is no specific age: what determines their placement is the availability of a space or carer in a setting".

Details about destinations are also mixed, and inevitably, we have been able to gather the most information from the countries who submitted the greatest number of questionnaires, as in these quite detailed composite responses from Spain first, then Israel and then Australia:

> It is difficult to find a suitable placement mainly due to the lack of availability and so many students stay home being cared for

by their parents/carers. Alternatively, they can attend a Centro de Día (Day Centre) if that´s what their family wants or go to a Transición para la Vida Adulta (Transition to Adult Life Centre) or to a Centros Ocupacionales (Occupational Centres) or to specific SEN [special educational needs] centres. Some may attend a class called 'Aula de promoción a la autonomía personal' (Class to encourage personal autonomy), but unfortunately some stay at home.

There are limited programs, and many are not very good, although there are a few excellent programs started by parents. Once they leave school, they tend to move to a vocational setting which often they are unable to participate in for lack of physical and cognitive skills and they do not continue to receive adequate physical and speech therapy in these settings. Often they go back home and live with their families or to residential care or supportive housing or to a hostel or assisted living in the community. Some do go to extracurricular activities like painting, listening to music and more.

After school, they tend to live at home with day program support, and one-on-one carers provided through National Disability Insurance Scheme (NDIS). They can also continue to access speech therapy, occupational therapy, music programs and respite care.

There is a similar, although not always well-resourced, provision in many other countries, with the mixture of "residential housing with day programs" reported in New York being echoed in Finland, Greece, Macedonia, Norway and Ireland, and these provide activities ranging from "structured leisure activities" in Greece to "group home settings with preparatory programmes for independent life" reported in Finland, although from Ireland, we hear that there are "not always spaces available, so many have to wait for a day service".

Only two respondents report that "there is no provision so young people with PMLD are normally at home", although in Kenya, we hear that they are placed in "private foster homes" and, in Thailand, that they either "stay at home with their families" or "while some of them stay in residential facilities for individuals with severe disabilities, some of them live with their families".

There is clearly then a wider issue here that for many young people with PMLD around the world; once they have left school, there is very little other option than returning to their families on a more or less full-time basis with no other provision available for them. One speech and language therapist in Singapore points out that this doesn't necessarily have to be a bad thing as "some families are great at encouraging their child to be more independent e.g. by providing communication opportunities, encouraging self-feeding/assistance with dressing etc", and a teacher in Singapore agrees that "for families with more familial support, they are sometimes able to continue to give and create opportunities for the students to be independent within their home environment". This more positive attitude to people with PMLD being at home after leaving school is not widespread amongst respondents to the survey, however, with a teacher trainer from Taiwan expressing the concern that "families tend to protect and are not willing to adapt" and the speech and language therapist and then a teacher from Singapore qualifying their earlier remarks as follows:

> Some families may find it easier to do everything for their child and not provide the opportunities.
> Most of the time, I think the students become more dependent after they leave school because it is easier for the caregivers to just take care of their basic needs (e.g. feed them instead of allowing them to feed themselves – less of a mess and faster).

A teacher in Greece sums up starkly so many of the responses to the question of how independent they can be: "most people with PMLD live with their parents or other family members until they die".

We have seen earlier from the UK context that practitioners generally feel that post-school provision is not able to build on or even match the support for wellbeing and independence offered in compulsory schooling, and this is certainly reflected in the international survey in which participants were asked directly about young people with PMLD: "after they have left school are they able to be more or less independent and why?" Many schools in many countries, as we have seen in the UK, do, of course, work hard to prepare these young people for the next stage in their lives, and it is important to acknowledge, of course, that to a certain extent success depends on individual circumstances or, in the words of a Spanish teacher, that "it mainly depends on the input from the school and specially the involvement of the family"; nevertheless, nearly 40% of respondents stated fairly unequivocally that they felt young people with PMLD were not able to be as independent once they have left school, although respondents from Spain and Singapore tend to be cautiously optimistic about post-school provision in their countries, reporting the following:

> The day centres they attend work at preparing them to be more independent, though unfortunately those who stay at home tend to lose it.
> They are more independent after they leave school. In school, we break down their tasks into smaller step and scaffold their learning towards honing skills that allows independence. Through school, parents also benefit from learning about adaptive devices and how they can support their child's learning at home.

A teacher in Australia however sees post-school independence as more of a necessity than the result of provision or policy reporting that "they have to be more independent [though more isolated as well] as they have less access to daily support and a community at school that has known them for the previous 15 years".

There are various reasons put forward to explain in more detail why these young people can become less independent after they have left school and why as one teacher from Spain puts it "their normalisation opportunities might diminish". Respondents in Israel, Ireland, Australia and New York put it down principally to similar discrepancies we have heard about in the UK between staffing ratios, resources and funding at school compared to services for adults whilst a researcher from Norway feels "their lives are often much more controlled after they leave school", and a student teacher expresses a very real concern that because of a lack of trained staff "the person has less independence and may be strapped to a chair".

Clearly then, in the UK and arguably more so in many other countries, there is a need to develop what one respondent calls "greater and more meaningful provision" for young people with PMLD once they have left school. This fact shouldn't, however, detract from the good practice that does already exist and to conclude this chapter we talked to David Bliss, who has worked in several school and post-19 environments in the UK and asked him a number of questions about what best practice and personalised provision might look like for young people with PMLD once they have left school. We have summarised his responses in the following:

How important are partnerships with the local schools and what represents good practice in terms of school/college collaboration and preparation for transition?

It is important to recognise that the voice of the young person with PMLD needs to be heard, and so, during the transition period which takes them beyond school, they should be given sufficient opportunities to speak in their unique ways, which, in turn, will help the post-19 provision – whatever that may be – to form a more accurate overview of who the young person is and what they want. So the school should provide opportunities for the incoming service provider to listen to the young person as much as possible. Best practice is, of course, one in which the young person is given the opportunity to try out the new provision over a number of years with their parents and carers fully involved as well. A young person with a good transition will have the benefit of the experience of where they are going, experience of the staff they will be working with and experience of peers they will be meeting, of sharing their aspirations, interests, needs and ways of working. In summary, the following factors are key to a successful transition:

- Dedicated staff members for transition in both the school and the college
- A good working relationship between the school and the college
- A transition process over as many years as possible
- Sharing paperwork

116 Part II

- Clear and effective communication passports which are interpretable (an easy read) and accessible (not too large or unwieldy)

- Regular planning meetings

- Opportunities for parents to visit and share input

When a young person is new to an area – which does sometimes happen, of course – there is inevitably a certain amount of guesswork because information for the previous school or other stakeholders may, in part, be missing.

What are some of the issues faced when 'the young people pass from child services to adult services'?

Leaving statutory education is a big step for all school leavers. For young people with PMLD, it may well be that for 14 years, their immediate support systems have been under the one group of services and that in the majority of cases, those services have established relationships with both the school the young person attends and their parents or carers. It is important to understand that for all of us, a balanced lifestyle is important to good wellbeing. For a young person with PMLD, moving from child to adult services significantly alters this balance in the short term, and we need to make sure we recognise that and plan for it so that it is manageable.

These are just a few of the factors which need to be taken into consideration in this transition:

- A different weekly routine with different start and end times

- New people and environments to get used to

- Different sensory stimuli such as smells and background noises to get used to

- A different transport provider

- Different respite opportunities

- Different health professionals who don't necessarily work in the same way

- Possibly different communication systems

- Different protocols and equipment for things like enteral feeding and physiotherapy

- Often the move from child to adult services can result in a reduction in respite care, meaning the young person spends more time at home with parents who are, at the same time, getting less support. There may also be potential changes to sources of funding.

How should provision post-19 nurture, maintain and generalise each student's unique skill set?

Nurturing a young person's skill set is about giving them the opportunities above all in a personalised way to engage and develop through 'learning moments'. It is also about understanding what the student and the parents want by allowing a profile of the young person to be built and then matching them to a learning programme which is individualised to meet their needs and nurture their skills. Recognising and celebrating learning is also essential to maintaining those skill sets as is matching the young person to an appropriate communication partner.

Some colleges use the word vocation to describe a key aim for each young person. What does vocation mean in this context?

Vocation can be work-related, of course, but in this context, vocation tends to mean hobbies or leisure activities, again as personalised as possible, so it is essential we find out what motivates a young person and then think of ways we can develop those things in a vocational context. The list is endless really: anything from arts and crafts, to gardening, recycling, dog walking, meeting new people, trainspotting, shopping, baking, cooking and so on.

What sort of skills do you think staff need to work in post-compulsory provision for this group?

Obviously, the skills to keep a young person safe and to use specific physiotherapy equipment or to use enteral feeding techniques, but just as important is how we listen to them and communicate effectively, receptively and expressively with them, with lots of opportunities to engage, to affect their own environment, to communicate and to be heard.

The staff working with these young people need to be a part of a supportive team led by someone with a clear vision for the young person which they can share with the team. There needs also to be a strong induction to ensure that staff can work effectively from the beginning, with a clear professional development plan.

What sort of assessment methods do you think are appropriate at this age?

Assessment needs to be linked to learning, which is student-led, or, in other words, learning for and with the student, rather than activities which are done to the student with a nice product at the end of the session. Individual learning opportunities should be identified by staff who work closely and consistently with the young person, and there needs to be a mechanism in place for this information to be shared. Assessment processes should also be constantly reviewed by the whole team around the child so that progress continues to develop. Achievements should be celebrated on a daily, weekly or termly basis. Finally, a clear record of their achievements is an important resource to share with other stakeholders, particularly when they go on beyond college to new services or new placements, and into their adult life.

What sort of future destinations after college and into adult life are there in the UK?

There are various day opportunities to choose from, which include services and communities which are run by established providers. They might also have personal assistants (PAs) who work individually with them. Other than this, some young people will access short breaks or respite opportunities as they did before with, and supported living is also a possible destination.

Day opportunities also allow a young person to meet and socialise with their peers, which can sometimes be in an area of vocational interest, for example a drama or music group. Ideally, the staff team around the young person should meet weekly to discuss and review the offer to the young person, that is to say, what is working and what is not working and what they might develop for the future.

Take the example of a young person whose parent was particularly involved and was very clear about the aspirations for her daughter throughout her time at college. She liked opportunities to socialise, she needed time to manage her posture, and she thrived on opportunities to control her environment, either through communication or assistive technology. This young person's parent didn't feel that there were any day opportunities suitable and instead hired and trained three personal assistants, and these PAs shadowed her at college to become familiar with how she worked best and specifically how she used assistive technology and how she should be positioned during her times out of her chair. She also got together with three other parents to hire a hydrotherapy pool at a local special school, after-school hours. On the college's part, her day was shortened to allow her the time to access this.

Other good practice might involve collaborative working on transition between both the daytime provision and the personal assistants so that the young person is supported in voicing an opinion on any possible daytime opportunities. This would also involve training, especially during which a young person uses assistive technology and the PAs or staff from day services would be trained in its use, with day opportunity providers involving themselves in the young person's EHC Plan reviews.

Supported living is an option for a young person at the age of 18, and it is a big transition. For a young person in supported living, the residential provider should ideally manage the young person's day when they are not accessing education. Where this works best is where there is a transition and collaborative working between the college, the supported living residence and the parents, carer and young person, whether in the form of shadowing the young person at college, being involved in their reviews or sharing skills and information between all stakeholders.

As an example, there was a young person who was on a short-term break of 4 weeks in supported living. Despite the short-term stay, they soon established and reviewed a routine that worked for the young person based on their needs and motivations. They adapted their bedroom and sleep routine. We observed that they were clearly happier and more content on arrival and throughout the day, and we passed this information onto the residential setting. On one occasion, the young person, upon arriving at college, clearly indicated that they wanted to return with the driver to their residential setting!

How can we monitor or track a student's progress once they have left college?

It is important for a post-19 college to have good relationships with the day providers and PAs or parent groups to allow for continued contact and – when necessary – input. This is an important question as a lot of parents say that the thing they would miss most on leaving college would be the contact with professionals.

David was particularly enthusiastic in his responses about the work of Chailey Heritage School as the learner is absolutely at the heart of everything the school does, and its entire approach is that anything is possible for every young person who is with the school, with its entire curriculum model built to support this. We will find out a lot more about the innovative personalised work of Chailey Heritage School in Part III.

Reference list

DfE. (2015). *Special educational needs and disability code of practice: 0–25 years.* London: HMSO.

The *Lives Lived Well* surveys
The link between policy and practice

We saw in Chapter 4 that the way wellbeing and independence are defined in national and international policy doesn't appear to support the needs of this group of learners. So in both the national and international *Lives Lived Well* surveys, we concluded by asking if teachers and practitioners felt the same: that educational policy did not adequately account for the needs of learners with PMLD. This was, of course, inspired a least, in part, by that phrase spoken by a headteacher at the original 2018 conference at Swiss Cottage, where it could be said this whole project started and which we mentioned in Chapter 5 that "although the *SEND Code of Practice* (2015) appears to 'cover' learners with PMLD, . . . it may not at the same time 'cater' for them", and we wanted to find out to what extent this sentiment was shared by practitioners around the world with reference to their own national policies regarding pupils with PMLD. As with the previous chapter, we will start with the UK context and then, unlike in Chapters 6 and 7, where responses from the international survey are integrated into a general discussion around wellbeing and independence, we treat country responses individually, starting with those countries – Spain, Israel and Australia for instance – which provided the largest amount of data in response to this question and then summarising responses across the other countries who responded in less detail to this question.

The UK context

Only 24 of the 52 respondents to the UK survey chose to answer the question, '*To what extent do you feel The SEND Code of Practice (2015) takes account of the needs of learners with PMLD aged 14–19 and why?'* although we recognise that this may partly have been because of 'survey fatigue' at the end of 26 questions! Of those 24 respondents, only 2 made positive statements about *The Special Educational Needs and Disabilities (SEND) Code of Practice* with relation to learners with PMLD, although it should be borne in mind here that the original UK survey very largely focused on learners in the 14–19 age range. One said that "there is advice and information about relevant websites", which is certainly true, with the 'References' section at the end of *The SEND Code of Practice* containing nearly 150 useful weblinks to guidance and policy documents on a chapter-by-chapter basis. The other positive comment was around the fact that young people with PMLD are now "deemed educable until 25" as well as support for the provision of personal budgets, which has meant this particular school has been able to design and implement "a much more flexible approach to after school provision".

However, there are many other unsubstantiated criticisms about whether *The SEND Code of Practice* takes account of the needs of learners with PMLD from the blunt: "it doesn't!" "not at all" and "it's almost as if they don't exist" to the slightly more forgiving "it just touches the surface" and the more general: "special schools are often an afterthought (in policy) and even more so for learners with pmld".

Some of the criticisms are more contextualised and, in particular, around the fact that the often very complex needs of these learners are not adequately taken into account:

> These learners needs are wide ranging and complicated and the SENCoP [*The SEND Code of Practice*] does not take account of that.
> I think the complexity of the needs of these learners is not necessarily recognised in this document. It is our job to adapt it to be suitable for them.
> I think it neglects to accept the complexities of this cohort in its provision.

Two respondents are concerned that the particular age group of 14 to 19, which was a focus of the UK survey, presents particular challenges for current policy "because they are coming to [the] end of their education provision" and are not "likely to succeed at college and in living independently". These and comments such as "conceptions of work devalue this group" echo again concerns expressed in the literature (e.g. Jordan, 2013) about discrepancies between conventional definitions of independence and the actual lives of people with PMLD and, in particular, the frequent conflation in policy of independence with employment.

Addressing some of the more detailed guidance in *The SEND Code of Practice*, the annual review process is seen by one respondent to have revealed "an irony in the fact that the new policy framework is supposed to benefit families but in fact has just revealed gaps in provision", with another suggesting that "provision varies across the country", and this is certainly an issue which we have heard more detail about in Chapter 8. The emphasis on SMART (specific, measurable, achievable, realistic, time-limited) targets within Education, Health and Care (EHC) Plans comes in for some criticism because this approach is "not always appropriate" and "it's hard to keep the soft skills on the agenda". Two respondents report that it is not uncommon for EHC Plans to be discontinued from the age of 19, meaning that sadly, the young people are "just left at home".

There is then an almost universal feeling that the *SEND Code of Practice* (2015), which is statutory guidance, does not adequately account for this group of learners, and the implications of this are likely to last some years as the gap between the previous *SEND Code of Practice* in 2001 and the current was 14 years. For many schools though "the Code of Practice is really just a guide to ensure we are doing the minimum legally in terms of educational protocol", and one school feels that the *PMLD Core and Essential Standards* discussed briefly in Part I are "a better representation" with another using these standards "as a way of evaluating the quality of the work that we do rather than as a planning tool". Other schools lean more on the Preparing for Adulthood (PfA) agenda from Year 9 onwards, although it, too, is not without its criticisms which are similar to those directed at *The SEND Code of Practice*:

> The preparing for adulthood materials are aimed at people with less complex needs and the outcomes are often unachievable for our cohort.

> The complexity of their lives isn't taken into account and (the PfA) doesn't recognise that need doesn't change at 19.

Policy in other countries

It is important here to reiterate something we said in Chapter 5 when we introduced the *Lives Lived Well* surveys. The UK survey, which ran from November 2019 to March 2020, was aimed specifically at teachers or leaders in schools who were authorised to teach young people with PMLD, with an emphasis in the 14–19 age range. The fact that about a quarter of all those schools responded to the survey means that the results can be said to be relatively representative of the sector as a whole. The international survey however employed initially what is known as 'convenience' sampling; in other words, the survey was sent to contacts we and others already had around the world and then, through 'snowball' sampling, those people passed the survey link on to others. This resulted in 66 responses from 19 countries with, in many cases, only one or two responses per country or state within that country. So we can make no claims to validity with respect to policy within each country. Nor were we able just to target teachers, and although, in reality, many of the respondents were teachers or schools leaders, we also received responses from people in other roles such as classroom assistants, speech and language therapists, psychologists, researchers and, of course, parents and carers. We were unable also to make a detailed analysis of policies existing in that country in the way we were able to in the UK, a setting we were of course already very familiar with. The opinions expressed in the following then about national policy are just that: personal opinions from a range of people who work with young people in their country with PMLD and need to be treated as such. We have not given as many details in this chapter about the job roles of the respondents to preserve anonymity still further.

Spain

Two of the 14 people from Spain who responded to the *Lives Lived Well* survey were broadly positive about education policy in their country with regard to young people with PMLD, stating that although they are "increasingly taken into account", it is only "in general terms" or "not in real terms" and that there should be more attention paid in policy to "the opinion of professionals and families who know the reality and the real needs they have".

As with responses from other countries, issues around inclusion in mainstream schools are often cited and far more so than in the UK, perhaps indicating, as we discussed in Chapter 6, that 'full inclusion' (Kauffman, Felder, Ahrbeck, Badar, & Schneiders, 2018) is still policy and a live issue for practitioners in many countries around the world. As an example of this, in Spain for instance, which embraces in spirit if not in policy the movement of *Plena inclusion*, come these heartfelt responses:

> It gives me shivers when a politician speaks of 'inclusive education', when not even special education schools have the necessary tools to offer an inclusive education, and even less mainstream schools, even when they have to cater for people with other disabilities.
>
> I am in favour of inclusion, but it is clear that in many cases it is not the most positive (option). There are students who because of their characteristics need the support of specialists or the use of resources which are only in the special schools. Inclusive Yes, but Special Too.
>
> Mainstream schools need more guidance and advice from special needs schools.

One respondent writing specifically about a particular region in Spain gives a cogent and compelling argument why the policy of inclusion may not have worked for learners with PMLD:

> We have gone from integration to inclusion without conducting an evaluative study of the policies implemented. I defend special schools as the most inclusive resource that exists for students with pmld. They employ specialized teachers and the basic resources necessary to carry out the teaching of learning for people´s global development. Without the existence of special schools, these people would be confined, as they were at the beginning of the last century, in their homes in the care of their relatives. The special

school is where proactive practices are carried out for the global development of the person with pmld, taking into account their uniqueness and individuality.

With respect to policy in general regarding young people with PMLD, the majority of responses from Spanish practitioners are fairly negative, with a focus on the poor provision of resources, which means that teachers have to fall back on "our own experiences and common sense", and in contrast to the UK for example, one respondent even suggests that "carers are better considered than the actual person with pmld".

Very much in line with what we saw in the UK survey, there are also a number of quite harsh and unsubstantiated criticisms of policy:

> We are always the forgotten ones.
> In my country disability is not taking into account in education.
> To be honest no one outside of what it is called 'normal' is taken into account.
> They are not taken into consideration in the policies nor in the community.
> The tendency is overprotecting as a way of freeing the State of responsibilities, considering that being cared for and fed should be enough.
> The educational policies are obsolete in relation to the advances that other countries are following.
> Legislative regulations for special education go back to the 1980s. Legislation has been made using 'patches' and inventing concepts that do not take into account the individual reality of people with pmld.

On a more positive note, however, the sheer number of responses from Spain and the enthusiasm for the *Lives Lived Well* survey point to a growing commitment to improving policy, or as one respondent puts it,

> These are things in which we need to get better at, to train and to raise awareness for all, and to promote their rights of people with pmld to achieve their inclusion.

Israel

Here again in Israel, respondents chose to address issues of inclusion under the theme of policy. One respondent interviewed three other teachers before completing the survey and all agreed that although "there are very good schools for students with pmld in Israel", they are at the same time uncomfortable with the fact that learners with PMLD are expected to follow the "regular national curriculum with certain adaptations", although one does acknowledge that "schools do have quite a lot of leeway". This, however, is not seen as going far enough, and many respondents from Israel lament that fact that "instead of communication being a main goal" of education for this group, subjects including geography, maths and Bible studies have to be taught, and while there is an acknowledgement that, for example, teaching about the world for this group can become "a lesson of feeling water", the overall feeling is expressed in the following:

> I just believe that we need to focus more on WHY we are teaching something, and less on WHAT we are teaching. . . . What about all the basic skills they are missing??

Australia

Australia presents an interesting contrast across the three Australian states represented in the survey responses. A respondent from Melbourne calls policy and provision for learners with PMLD "pretty amazing really" and goes on to explain that what are known as 'Special Developmental Schools' create "as optimal as possible a space for our students with pmld", concluding with "I'm pretty proud to be a part of it".

A respondent writing about Victoria and Queensland presents a very different picture and one more in line with some of the highly critical responses to policy we have seen before in the UK and elsewhere:

> The people who write policy have no idea of the life experience of the learner with pmld or their family. Policy is developed by political groups and individuals and it filters down. Those with-

out a voice are forced to endure the policy. Inclusion is a very misunderstood concept in Australia: It is assumed to mean that everyone gets the same provision rather than equality of opportunity. The country has an 'inclusive' curriculum which results in students with pmld enduring the same curriculum items as mainstream.

Intriguingly, this respondent then goes on to mention the cricketer 'Donald Bradman' as an example of a topic which is covered on the regular curriculum and therefore by those with PMLD as well!

Of the other countries represented in the *Lives Lived Well* survey, most do not feel that policy takes account of learners with PMLD, although, of course, in some countries, such as for instance the US, that policy "depends on each individual school district".

Responses from practitioners in countries designated as 'lower middle income' by the World Bank explain that economic factors mean that these countries (in this case Timor Leste) "struggle to include all children with disabilities, but those with more complex needs are particularly disadvantaged". A response from Kenya also talks about "institutional barriers" and the fact that "the agenda on disability is not a high priority in parliament". Because of this, steps have not been taken by health and social services to overcome "the environmental barriers learners with pmld face". Some special schools in Kenya, explains this respondent, are still "stuck within the medical model of disability, and are simply classified as schools for either the physically handicapped or the mentally challenged".

The respondents from Hungary, Greece, Slovakia, Macedonia, Florida in the US and one of the Finnish participants simply say 'No' to the question of whether learners with PMLD are taken into account in policy in their countries. Others feel more or less the same but back up their response with some explanation or context. In Thailand for instance, where it is apparently "compulsory to include pupils with pmld in regular schools" and legally they have "equal rights to receive support services based on individual's needs", these good intentions are mitigated by "many factors which influence the development of education as well as quality of life of individuals with severe disabilities", and there is a "lack of teachers that understand how to help people this group".

Generally speaking, there is a sense in the responses that young people with PMLD are overlooked even where policy favours full inclusion, and it is, as one respondent from the US explains, "up to the people who are around them to advocate for them". This is echoed by a response from Finland, where "this group of people tend to stay in the shadow of others with less severe learning difficulties", and even where schools and practices are encouraged to be more inclusive, "this minority group of pupils is forgotten and set aside. They are not seen or considered being able to be a natural part of an inclusive school".

A lack of funding is cited by a respondent in Cyprus as being a major contributory factor to the perceived low status of these young people in policy: "I think they are completely neglected as they think that they are burdens on the society who take money out of the social welfare system", and in Ireland, too, "they are not seen as a priority here and government continues to pull back on funding".

A few of the people who answered this question present a more hopeful picture and, in particular, those from India. The response from a researcher in Norway also acknowledges that national policy does take account of those with PMLD, although "there is always a bit of a gap between policy and practice and I think we have room for improvement".

Improvements are also recognised by a teacher trainer in Taiwan, where there is now "a chance to support our learners with pmld to exercise self-determination", and in France, where although there has been no acknowledgement in policy previously, "there is now a political support, so we hope that the schooling of people with pimd will increase, and that the training of professionals will be more and more suitable".

Despite these perceived failings of statutory policy around the world, what has come across throughout the analysis of the data drawn from the *Lives Lived Well* surveys in the previous chapters is the commitment and sheer hard work schools devote to the wellbeing and independence of this group of young people, summed up I think by this from one of the UK respondents:

> We do this because of a firmly held belief that it is not simply what our pupils learn, but the manner in which they learn it that determines how successful they are once they leave school.

So, in Part I, we have discussed how wellbeing and independence have been defined and discussed by researchers and writers in the field, in Part II, we have heard from teachers, parents and other practitioners from around the world about how they seek to enhance the wellbeing and independence of this group and some of the barriers they face in doing this. For Part III, we now turn to Chailey Heritage School in Sussex to find out in a very real and practical way how they work from day to day in the classroom and beyond with their learners with PMLD.

Reference list

DfE. (2015). *Special educational needs and disability code of practice: 0–25 years.* London: HMSO.

Jordan, R. (2013). *Autism with severe learning difficulties* (2nd ed.). London: Souvenir Press.

Kauffman, J. M., Felder, M., Ahrbeck, B., Badar, J., & Schneiders, K. (2018). Inclusion of all students in general education? International appeal for a more temperate approach to inclusion. *Journal of International Special Needs Education, 21*(2), 1–10.

PART III
Focus on Chailey Heritage School

10 Welcome to Chailey Heritage School!

Introduction

This concluding part of the book explains how the theory described in Part I, and the practice discussed in Part II, has been translated into a pragmatic approach at Chailey Heritage School to improve the lives of young people including those with profound and multiple learning difficulties (PMLD). It describes how both areas (wellbeing and independence) have been interpreted into meaningful practice in the 'real' world.

As anyone working in the field will know, we do not start working on these aspects at 14; therefore, we discuss how these are encouraged from day 1, nurturing and encouraging young people to fulfil their own potential. We also explain how we prepare and support our eldest pupils through the transition into new settings. The intention is for this part of the book to demonstrate the innovative nature of a personal curriculum and how we support each and every young person to fulfil their potential as well as being inspirational in nature. It does not suggest that 'one size fits all,' and professionals should decide for themselves what is relevant to their own cohort of students and what is not. This section has been written by practitioners with a specialty in PMLD who work, or have worked, with these students as well as other children and young people with a range of cognitive abilities. It will involve some case studies of young people with a variety of cognitive levels, predominantly, but not exclusively, those with profound and multiple learning difficulties.

Our history

Chailey Heritage was founded in 1903 by a very determined lady named Grace Kimmins who wore a very distinctive purple dress. Her dream was to create the same opportunities for those, 'whom society provided nothing'. To commemorate this, and to consolidate her place in Chailey history, the colour of the foundation was changed to the same purple she wore. What she created was the first

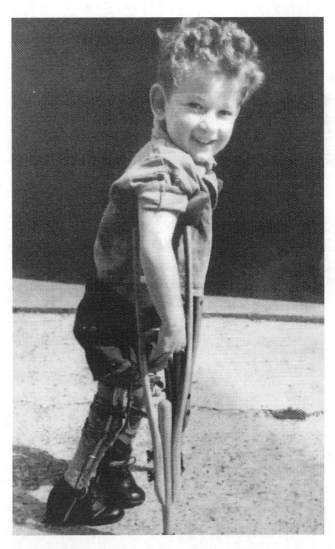

Figure 10.1 Historic pictures of children at Chailey Heritage

Welcome to Chailey Heritage School! **135**

Figure 10.2 Historic pictures of children at Chailey Heritage

purpose-built public school in the country for children with disabilities. We do not go into the history or background of Chailey Heritage too much as there are already some excellent books listed in the references that do this; instead, I signpost them here: *Grace Kimmins and Her Chailey Heritage, Chailey Heritage: A Hundred Years* and *My Grandmother's Footsteps* written by Grace Kimmins's granddaughter, Verena Hanbury MBE.

When we look back at the history, it is clear that much has changed in the way children with a disability are viewed and how special schools operate. Grace Kimmins was ahead of her time when it came to trying to improve their lives, even though the methods may now seem unusual. The language used and the needs of the children have changed significantly, as have the practices. What was seen at the time as transformational has continued not only to evolve and change to reflect the times but also to lead the way, with the continued involvement of the descendants of Grace Kimmins. The young people who Carpenter et al. (2011) describe as presenting with different profiles of learning for which the teaching profession is not pedagogically prepared, now make up the majority of our cohort of students.

The Chailey Heritage Foundation (CHF) now comprises the following:

- The school – a non-maintained 'outstanding' Office for Standards in Education (Ofsted)–graded special school

- A residential provision which offers a range of packages from short breaks, respite and 52-week boarding

- Chailey Heritage Pathways – specialised care and support both at home and in the community

- The Life Skills Centre – a learning environment for those 16 and older

- The Hub – a young-adult transition service, from 16 which offers social activities as well as activities and support for health and wellbeing

- The Futures Hub – where young adults 19 to 30 years with complex physical and sensory needs can socialise, pursue and develop interests, and use the facilities for leisure and life skills

To find out more explore www.chf.org.uk.

Our pupils

Throughout this section, we refer to the pupils in school as 'young people' for ease of writing, although this will encompass all ages from nursery to 19, as well as considering those in our 19- to 30-year-old provision.

Welcome to Chailey Heritage School! 137

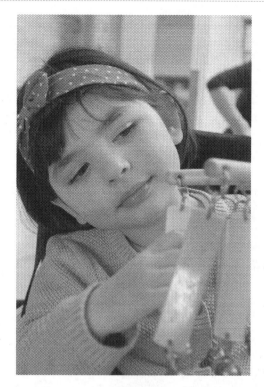

Figure 10.3a C a pupil at Chailey Heritage

Figure 10.3b F a pupil at Chailey Heritage with Debbie, a member of staff

Young people who come to Chailey Heritage School have several things in common; first and most important, they are children and young people. They have the same rights as their non-disabled peers, even if it is more complicated and more costly to support those rights. They all have a physical disability and have the need for wheelchairs for all, or the majority, of the time. The other thing these young people have in common is that they all have complex medical conditions that cannot be accommodated in a school without medical support. This includes young people on ventilators, those who have uncontrolled epilepsy and those who need enteral feeding, catheterisation and have many other medical needs requiring interventions.

The majority also have sensory needs. They may have a degree of visual or hearing loss or in some cases be 'deafblind', therefore having no hearing or vision with which to interpret the world.

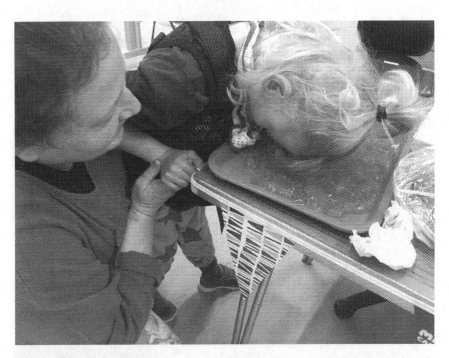

Figure 10.4 L - a deaf blind learner exploring jelly

Source: Image by permission of Chailey Heritage Foundation www.chf.org.uk.

'L' is deafblind and likes to explore using his head and face. He is supported here by an intervenor, someone trained specifically to support the wellbeing and independence of those children who are deafblind.

What sets them apart from some other children in most other special schools is that they have a range of cognitive abilities, from those children whose other difficulties, make it more difficult to learn to those who have profound learning difficulties as well as physical, sensory and medical difficulties.

Our approach

The philosophy which underpins everything at Chailey Heritage Foundation (CHF) is care and respect for everyone with high regard and support for wellbeing and independence. Our vision is a society where individuals of all abilities are valued and no one is excluded because of their disability. Our mission is to give disabled children and young people every opportunity to pursue their full potential. As mentioned previously, our pupils are recognised as children first, with the same needs, wishes, wants and aspirations as any other child. Then we take into account their individual interests and preferences as well as physical, sensory and medical needs to support them to learn, have fun and be as physically active as possible.

Medical and care needs are done *with* and not *to* the young person whilst taking into account their feelings and comfort. What underpins everything is support for their wellbeing and independence throughout. Medical tasks are also completed along with something more fun to ensure that the focus is on being a child and not someone needing constant medical treatment, even if they do. Young people at CHF are amongst the most medically complex in the country, they require medical care and interventions throughout the day.

Specialist staff

Our staff are trained by nurses to take over as many medical tasks as they are allowed to do as well as completing training on every aspect of care and education they may come across. They can also work towards

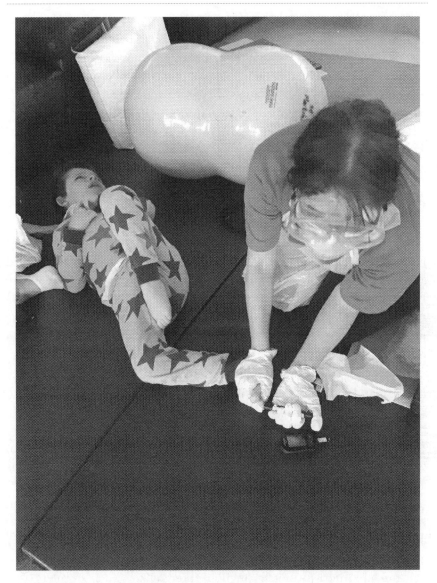

Figure 10.5 A nurse completing a medical task

Specialist Educational Assistant accreditation. With an emphasis on teachers' expertise within the curriculum, which is discussed later, it follows that a lot of time and thought also goes into their professional development and support. When teachers begin working with us, they are given a mentor. Each teacher is expected to undertake their own learning, developing their expertise in areas of interest or need and then disseminating it. For example, if they have a child with Rett's syndrome or Angelman's syndrome in their class, there is an expectation that they will become knowledgeable and share that expertise. They are also encouraged to undertake other professional qualifications which enhance their understanding, at a variety of levels. This has led to a cohort of teachers with a wide range of expertise who support one another.

As a school, we regularly support teachers of students with PMLD from schools around the country who ask for help because their senior leadership team 'do not understand' how teaching and learning happen for these students. Some believe that PMLD students just require a simpler version of what other more able students require, or they are simply expected to experience what others participate in. We would argue that they need a separate and distinct pedagogy (Imray & Hinchliffe, 2014) and staff with particular expertise. Contrary to popular belief, this is not easier than other forms of teaching but, if done correctly, is just as challenging and is a specialty which is vastly underrated. There is also an interesting question to answer here about whether teachers who specialise in teaching those with PMLD are in senior leadership positions. An interesting research project perhaps?

In order to manage the range of cognitive differences, a variety of strategies are used, each one rooted in theory, research and appropriate pedagogy. Underpinning all this is the belief that *all* children, whatever their disability, should have the opportunity to develop their potential in all areas of their lives.

At the curriculum level, we have developed a completely personal curriculum based on each individual child. At the beginning of the process, there was a determination that those young people with PMLD were going to be as much of a priority as any other learner, as the authors believe that they are often forgotten, are considered too difficult to cater to or the teaching expertise is lacking. In some special schools, with a mixed cohort of students, including those who are physically mobile and active and those with a physical disability, it is obvious that those who are more active and more likely to need intervention are going to become the priority for stretched staff. This is not a criticism; it is simply an observation of how it is, and many of us have been in that situation. But my assertion at this point is that it does not support the wellbeing or independence of those young people with PMLD. These young people are already in danger of developing learned helplessness (Miller and Seligman, 1975), and then they are put into a position that makes this even more likely. They are also more vulnerable when in a mixed group of those in wheelchairs and those without, especially when they cannot move themselves away or are lying on the floor whilst others are running around.

As a non-maintained special school with on-site medical care and expertise in the support of young people with a severe physical disability, we do not take those who are more mobile. Therefore, we are in a unique position to comment; however, we are aware that local authority special schools do not have that choice. In the following chapters, we look at how the approaches at Chailey Heritage support the wellbeing and independence of every one of our young people.

Reference list

Arscott, D. (2003). *Chailey heritage: A hundred years.* Seaford: SB Publications.

Black, R. (2017). *Grace Kimmins and her Chailey heritage.* London: Arbe Publications.

Carpenter, B., Egerton, J., Bloom, T., Cockbill, B., Fotheringham, J. H., & Thistlethawaite, J. (2011). *The complex learning difficulties and disabilities research project: Developing pathways to personalised learning.* London: SSAT.

Hanbury, V. (as yet unpublished) Grandmother's Footsteps.

Imray, P., & Hinchcliffe, V. (2014). *Curricula for teaching children and young people with severe and profound and multiple learning difficulties; Practical strategies for educational professionals.* London: Routledge.

Miller, W.R., Seligman, M.E. (1975). Depression and Leanred helplessness in man. *Journal of Abnormal Psycholoby,* 84(3), 228–238.

Supporting wellbeing at Chailey Heritage School

Just like anything else you might see at Chailey Heritage, supporting wellbeing and independence requires a personal approach, as well as a strong ethos of care, respect and dignity. As a team, we consider the needs of each young person individually. As we consider their physical, medical and emotional needs, we also consider what learning will enhance their lives, contributing to their sense of wellbeing and independence. Supporting them to have as much control as possible over their own lives. We look at where their learning needs to start, what is next for them, and how it can best be achieved for every area of their lives.

Wellbeing at Chailey Heritage

In the classroom, young people are treated with dignity and respect as their communication is acknowledged and responded to. They are not rushed at any time during the day as everything is considered a learning opportunity; therefore, there is no rush to get back to the 'classroom learning'. All young people are supported to actively participate in *everything* they do. For example during trike riding, they are supported to push the pedals themselves, not be dragged around on a bike. During art activities, which are carefully chosen, the young people do as much of it as possible. During cooking sessions, they sometimes don't get further than exploring the ingredients as the focus is very much on the process, not the finished product. This is the difference between supporting access and supporting participation when a young person

144 Focus on Chailey Heritage School

with profound and multiple learning difficulties (PMLD) is really participating. Time is made to be in the moment with them, supporting them as much as possible to take the lead. Routines are structured so that they can be anticipated in the belief that anticipation leads to participation.

Wellbeing for us means the following:

- Ensuring the young people are as well as possible, not in pain, and comfortable in any of their equipment: walkers, chairs, standers or trikes

- Ensuring that the young people are settled in their environment and have developed attachments and trusting relationships with the people who care for them

- Ensuring that they have a voice, in whatever form that takes, and that they are listened to

- Being physically active which can have mental as well as physical benefits

- Supporting the young people to have control over their own lives, in whatever form this takes (this is discussed more in the next chapter)

- Providing an appropriate curriculum based around what that young person can do and ensuring that they have the best support to make progress

- Providing opportunities to take part in the same activities as their non-disabled peers

- Having fun and enjoying life

The Chailey Heritage Individual Learner Driven (CHILD) Curriculum

Whilst this section of the book is not a discussion about curriculum, at Chailey, the CHILD curriculum is an integral part of what makes us different from some other schools and has a direct bearing on the well-

Wellbeing at Chailey Heritage School 145

Figure 11.1 C enjoying the sound beam (a musical instrument activated by movement)

being, independence and community participation of all our pupils. As the authors have mentioned in other sections of the book, there is little research on the support of these elements for young people with PMLD and even less within policy. This leaves practitioners leading the way, interpreting what is best for our PMLD learners for themselves. Therefore, we must empower both the practitioners and the learners and contribute to the changes we want to see.

Background

In the 1990s, teachers in the UK felt obliged to teach the National Curriculum to pupils with PMLD. Many school leaders insisted on this as they feared being accused of segregation if they didn't. This led to a tension between the 'curriculum' and 'real' learning. In the classroom, young people would be 'experiencing' topics such as Florence Nightingale or the Romans, and the real learning, such as using a spoon and getting undressed or using the toilet, was not acknowledged. A teacher would feel that progress had been good, but when assessed against the UK National Curriculum P levels, it appeared that the young person had learned nothing.

For those outside the UK, the P levels were a set of descriptors used to assess the achievement of young people with SEN (special educational needs), who were working towards the first level of the National Curriculum. They were split into eight different levels, and young people with PMLD were those assessed between P1 and P3. However, the P scales have been widely criticised for a number of reasons, not least of which is that they were not very detailed and did not take into account physical or sensory difficulties. Today, the UK government has removed P levels, preferring instead to use engagement for assessment. There are problems with this too, but that discussion is for another day. Those of us working in special schools in the UK are now in the position where we can decide what curricula and method of assessment are best for our pupils. As often happens in education, the pendulum has swung in the other direction.

During 2014/2015, many special schools were still using the National Curriculum, but a few other schools were suggesting different learning paths for different learners. Dr Penny Lacey, who at the time was course leader for the master's in SPMLD (severe profound and multiple learning difficulties) that the authors were completing, visited Chailey Heritage to support this development. Penny pointed out the work that had been done at Castle Wood school in Coventry, in the UK, where she would spend 1 day a week working with the children. In terms of what we wanted to achieve, this perhaps was the closest. However, it was still not inclusive of our more cognitively 'able' learners.

The CHILD curriculum started as an action research project, to develop a 'fit for purpose' curriculum for *all* our learners. As discussed before, young people are placed with us because of their physical disability and need for on-site medical care. This means that nurses and doctors are available when there is an emergency or a change in health status which requires immediate attention. However, complex medical needs and a physical disability are not always associated with a severe or profound learning difficulty. So the challenge was to find a curriculum which could accommodate all of our learners, from those with a PMLD to those who find it more difficult to learn due to their physical, medical and sensory difficulties, as well as everyone in between.

It was at this point, that we decided to turn everything upside down and focus on the young person first and design individual, or personal curricula around them. It could then encompass very personal targets (we call them STEPs) that would not necessarily be relevant to another learner. Those of us who work in special schools know very well that what is relevant to one student may not be relevant to another.

Our headteacher, Simon Yates, often tells the story of one young lady who was terrified of dogs. Consequently, this made it incredibly hard for her parents to take her out and became the focus of any trip, causing enormous stress to her and her family. So a 'step' for her was to be introduced to, and eventually become relaxed around, dogs. This increased her wellbeing and that of her family, as well as making community participation possible. Another young person would become extremely distressed whenever he entered a café with his parents. So the on-site café and a local garden centre were used to help him learn to relax in that setting. Being relaxed when meeting a dog or visiting a

148 Focus on Chailey Heritage School

café certainly has a bearing on wellbeing, and enabling them to be part of family trips has made a huge difference. We know that many special schools work on these kinds of targets, but often it can become an 'add-on' to the 'educational' work done. We would argue that this is where the focus should be. We now explain how the CHILD curriculum works and how it supports the wellbeing, independence and community participation of all the young people at Chailey.

The CHILD curriculum has a set of personal core profiles for every important area of a young person's life, which are also matched with the areas of the Education, Health and Care (EHC) Plan. They include a baseline of where the young person is currently. These incorporate both long-term outcomes and 'My Next Steps' (MNS) for learning, anything which will enhance their wellbeing, independence or community participation.

Profiles include a description of prior achievement as well as advice on best practice strategies and requirements for the learning environment and activities to promote effective and meaningful learning. Penny Lacey (2007) would have said find out where the child is and don't leave them there!

The profiles are co-produced by the teacher, relevant therapists, parents and the young person. This ensures that the young person's aspirations, and, if appropriate, their parents, are included. A specialist teacher is also available to support, and all teachers support one another with a dialogue about how to write steps. There are also 'expert' (more experienced or qualified) teachers to support profound and multiple learning difficulties, multisensory impairment and specific learning (see the following discussion).

To baseline we use the following:

- Information from parent and family consultation, including home visits, and the child themselves if they are able to contribute

- Written documents from parents

- Any documents provided by previous schools/teachers, therapists and other specialists

- Any up-to-date advice that had been prepared for EHC Plans

- Assessment information from clinical services assessments, including nurses, doctors, speech and language therapists, occupational therapists (OTs), physios, behaviour support specialists, dieticians and so on

■ Assessment information from school assessment, including, as appropriate, sensory impairment specialist teacher; SPMLD specialist teacher; subject-specific lead teacher; Early Years Foundation Stage lead teacher; personal, social, health and economic/sex and reproduction education lead teacher

■ Observations

■ Anything else which may be useful

The acronym **STEP** stands for the following:

Specific – they should be clear and easy to assess
Tiny – our students make the best progress when steps are tiny
Emerging – it should be something we are starting to see, an emerging skill
Personal – it is not taken from a predetermined bank of targets; it might apply to just one child

Teachers are also given the following advice when writing 'Next Steps'

■ Is it meaningful and manageable? Ask yourself, **Why** is this important? **What** do I want to see? **Will** it make a positive difference in their lives? **Will** we be able to work on it regularly? **Will** I know when they have achieved it? This is where knowing your baseline is so important; if you know where the child has started, you will know when they have made progress. Clearly Penny Lacey's enduring influence is present here.

■ Ask yourself, is this a long-term target, is it more than one target or is it a target for us? Example: to use my walker three times a week (the child is reliant on you to help them into their walker, so this is a target for us!)

150 Focus on Chailey Heritage School

- Ensure you understand the student's sensory/engagement profile and that you aren't asking them to do something they can't do because of visual impairment (VI), hearing impairment (HI) or multisensory impairment (MSI), for example to do something which requires visual or auditory skills they do not have.

- Ensure that you are working on sensory MNS – visual, auditory, somatosensory (touch), proprioceptive, vestibular, gustatory, olfactory. Example: To fix on and follow an object when it is moving.

- Do not have too many MSN; you should be able to cover nearly all the MNS every week. If you have too many, slim them down.

- A Next Step should be an **emerging** skill (something you have already seen).

- Be clear where the student is now, this will make it easier to judge if an MNS has been achieved. The information *'I can do this . . .'* should be on the profiles – then it makes it obvious why they are working on the next or following step.

- Pitch your MNS carefully, particularly for students with PMLD. They may only have a few MNS, and this can really focus the learning. Also look at the MNS achieved, especially when you get a new pupil/class.

- Don't forget to add what kind of support you expect them to need in the profile as progress can be made when it is removed or they have less support.

- Be wary of using the word *consistent*, especially in choice making. How many of us are consistent about the things we like or in the responses we show? We might like something one day but not be that bothered with it another day. It may also depend on whether they have just had their medication or a particular time of day.

- Be careful with your use of language – for example 'to tolerate' – does it sound better to say to 'remain comfortable'. If they are tolerating it, think carefully about whether it is something that they need to do.

- Does the way it's written make it sound as if they are much more able than they are? Also, is it very broad so they will have to go through multiple steps to achieve it?

- Ensure it is an MNS and not an activity.

- Be Specific – the S of MNS

In this and the following chapter, we give examples of the profiles and discuss how they support the wellbeing, independence and community participation of our learners. Each of the profiles that follow is of a different young person and gives an idea of what can be covered in each.

It's important to clarify here that there is no bank or database of steps. This was done deliberately for several reasons. It is easy to quickly choose from a prewritten bank of steps without thought or reflection. We were also clear that we did not want to design yet another prescriptive curriculum. Instead, we wanted to empower teachers and acknowledge their expertise, as well as their knowledge of that young person. We wanted teachers to think carefully with other professionals and parents about what is important to that individual young person, for now and in the future. In other words, we have 'flipped the narrative' from teachers applying the same curriculum to all children to teachers learning about the individual child and developing expertise and strategies to support them, putting the child firmly in the centre.

Assessment

Assessment is ipsative and narrative rather than numerical or comparative. This means assessing the student against their starting point which, as mentioned earlier, Penny Lacey (2007) would call starting where the learner is. Comparisons are not made because, as Imray and Hinchcliffe (2014) point out, to compare would be like comparing apples and oranges, both equally good, but different. Comparing our young people serves no purpose as we can show the learning profile and story of progress for each one. It also ensures that each is equally important, which as we have previously stated was something we set out to do. Assessment consists of observations which are recorded on sticky notes and filed into each young person's area of the Class Assessment File of Evidence (CAFÉ). The teacher will determine when a young person has achieved a particular step and then set a new step.

152 Focus on Chailey Heritage School

'Next Steps' should not continue for years; if they go on too long, it's the wrong target, or it is too big. They are reviewed formally every 6 months but should be reviewed more regularly. When filling in the CAFÉ which is done weekly, it is useful to see when there is evidence and the child needs to be moved on. It is at the teacher's discretion when this happens. It is very important for the teacher to file the sticky notes, as it is a useful part of formative assessment. It's also useful to assess the quality of observation writing for Special Education Assistant appraisal, thus supporting their development too.

The following section shares some real-life anonymised examples of profiles. There are seven core profiles:

- Engagement and Sensory Support Profile

- Communication Profile

- Social and Emotional Wellbeing Profile

- Physical Profile

- Access Technology Profile

- A Driving Profile

- A Functional Skills Profile

There is also a specific learning profile which is relevant to some young people.

Each of the following profiles is from a different learner and are not all from PMLD learners.

Profile 1 – the engagement and sensory support profile

This profile incorporates medical, postural and sensory information which can have an impact on learning in the classroom. It supports the development of visual and auditory skills as well as encouraging attention and concentration. Sensory information is supported in school by two qualified MSI teachers who have access to clinic notes, attend audiology and ophthalmology clinics for the child and interpret these into a useable form for others.

Wellbeing at Chailey Heritage School 153

ENGAGEMENT & SENSORY SUPPORT PROFILE FOR ***** TEACHER: *****	
I am Multisensory impaired/Visually Impaired/Hearing Impaired	
The seven aspects of engagement: responsiveness; curiosity; discovery; anticipation; persistence; initiation; investigation.	
Pic here	**My current attention and concentration:**
	I am able to engage in motivating activities for sustained periods. I can persist with a task for up to 20 minutes, sometimes longer if I am really interested. I respond well to familiar people and familiar activities. I am curious about the environment around me and need time to explore it fully. I am working on anticipating elements of familiar routine such as the hello and goodbye routines. I am able to alert to a visual stimulus at close proximity and will reach out and grasp it if it is something of interest. However, my residual vision can be variable so help me to understand what I am seeing by using consistent language and give me time to explore. I tend to be alert to a visual stimulus better in a dark environment where there is little other visual distraction.
	Long-term outcomes for attention and concentration from Education and Health Care Plan
	Engage in play and learning activities that are differentiated to meet my needs as a learner who is multisensory impaired, in order to develop play and early learning skills
	Long-term outcomes for attention and concentration:
	▪ To engage in an increasing range of activities ▪ To attend to a task for extended periods of time ▪ To show persistence with a motivating task ▪ To make use of my residual vision and hearing to help me understand my environment and gain information
	Next steps for attention and concentration:
	E1 To use my hands in more complex ways during supported play **E2** To engage in an activity when sitting on the floor for 5 minutes. **E3** To show a preference for particular sounds or music. **E4** To track a visual stimulus left and right at close proximity (the letters and numbers above are only used to support filing; they are not provided for any other reason)

How to support my attention and concentration:

- I am a dual-impaired learner which means that the most important way you can support my attention and concentration is by making sure that I am working with an intervenor*

- My intervener also needs to be able to recognise and respond to my complex seizures and understand how my seizures affect my learning and general well-being. I need my day to follow a familiar structure and have consistent routines.

- I need activities to be repeated many times.

- I need adults to communicate with me through my personalised touch cues.

Medical/health issues that impact learning:

- I have multiple medical needs* which affect how I am feeling
  (*I have Complex de novo unbalanced chromosomal 16 anomaly, Complex Epilepsy (Vagal Nerve Stimulator [VNS] implanted), Multisensory impairment – visual and hearing impairment (bilateral hearing aids), Global developmental delay, Partly corrected cleft lip and palate, Cardiac disease (pacemaker), Gastroesophageal reflux disease, Gastrostomy)

- I have various levels of seizure activity – please check my seizure profile.

- I have my blended diet and my medication through my gastrostomy tube.

- I have a VNS fitted on the left side of my body – this is currently turned off.

- I also have a pacemaker on the right side of my body. I must be kept 6 inches away from WIFI as this can interfere with my pacemaker.

Postural management and implications for learning:

- I am able to move around independently on the floor by rolling and I can get myself up into a standing position. I can take some independent steps but I can only walk for very short distances and need support to do so.

How I see and implications for learning:

- I am visually impaired. Electrophysiology tests have shown some potential for vision. I alert to light toys in the sensory room.

Wellbeing at Chailey Heritage School **155**

- I can see when buttons light up. I appear to have more vision in the peripheral and lower peripheral areas.
- If I am stood up I cannot see the floor and I need help to avoid tripping over objects in my way.
- Sometimes I like to lie with my head upside down and this appears to be a strategy that I have learnt to use to help me to see better.

How I hear and implications for learning:

- I have sensorineural hearing loss and I wear bilateral hearing aids. I sometimes find it difficult to tolerate my hearing aids but this is improving. Please make sure my hearing aids are fitted properly, are not whistling and that they are free from condensation and wax.
- I have severe to moderate hearing loss across the sound fields.

How I touch/move and implications for learning:

- I like to explore my environment and test things out with my head (please keep me safe while I am exploring).
- I am able to touch with my hands and feet and like to explore things with my mouth.
- I am able to move around my environment by rolling, standing, walking short distances with support and close supervision. I like to taste things in my mouth (please follow my eating and drinking recommendations for this).

Ideas for sensory activities:

- Visual stimulation activities in the dark room or sensory studio.
- Listening and interaction games in the dark so that I can focus on listening.
- Tactile exploration of contrasting textures & media.
- Vestibular activities including twirling in a powered chair, rocking and spinning activities (using peanut ball, overhead hoist, roundabout, swing, hammock etc.).
- Body awareness activities including squashing & wrapping (following OT advice), massage, supported movement rhymes, Tac Pac (Communication through Touch).

*An intervenor is someone who has received specialised training to work with people who are deafblind. They facilitate exploration of the environment, support the learner's communication and promote their emotional wellbeing.

Profile 2 – the communication profile

Communication is a high priority and is explored more in the next chapter. It is important not to assume that all children who are non-verbal and have a severe physical disability have PMLD when they are 'locked in' or just not understood. This does happen, as the case of Jonathan Bryan (2018) demonstrates. Jonathan is a young man who was 'locked in,' but because he was not understood, he was considered a student with PMLD. This underlines two things, amongst others: the need for teachers to have developed their expertise so that they can recognise learners who may be locked in and the need to get to know the young person really well over time. It terrifies me that children can be taught without any prior training or expertise other than mainstream teacher education, which did little to prepare me for teaching in a special school. Equally, it terrifies me that some children are trying to

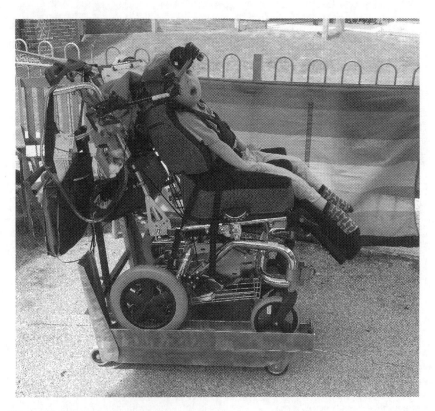

Figure 11.2 Little B driving the platform

communicate and being ignored, leading them to give up. I currently have a little boy in my class who is a perfect example of this.

When you first meet B, the uninitiated would see a little boy with PMLD who cannot move or speak and has a cortical visual impairment. However, B has the most wonderful sense of humour and good understanding. He loves Harry Potter and animals and works hard and uses inventive ways to get his message across. B has a communication book, but it is limited. In order to support his communication, as well as his wellbeing and independence, and after discussions with the speech and language therapist, we have to sometimes guess what he wants to talk about. We wouldn't advocate this in every situation as with some children it is easy to put words into their mouths. However, with B, this is not the case and not only enhances his wellbeing, as we find out what he wants to say, but also supports his independence as we support him to express himself so that it can be written down, shared and acted on. It is very important to B that it is written down as he worries that people will forget, and with him having worked so hard to get his message across, it's important that we don't!

Equally, it would be wrong of us to assume that all children are locked in when they may not be. Instead, it is up to us as teachers to unlock the potential that is there, and it is a serious responsibility and requires expertise. It is also the greatest reward a teacher can have and is another reason I, and other teachers, like me, do the job.

COMMUNICATION PROFILE FOR PUPIL:	
Teacher: SALT:	
	Long-term outcomes for communication from EHC Plan:
	■ To tolerate hand under hand support to position my hands into signs "more" and "stop" in appropriate contexts.
	■ To be able to copy vowel sounds an adult makes during intensive interaction.

	Long-term outcomes for communication:
	▓ To be able to communicate my interests, wishes and needs in a way that can be understood by people in my everyday life
	▓ To express how I am feeling in a way that can be understood by others
	▓ To be able to predict and understand what is happening next in my day
	Next steps for communication:
	C1 To engage with objects of reference (objects attached to photographs), which are presented immediately before an event starts
	C2 To take turns with a motivating item 1:1 with an adult
	C3 To follow the instruction 'stop' with verbal and visual support

My understanding of communication and implications for learning:

▓ Since my eyesight has improved, I have begun taking much more notice of people including their facial expressions.

▓ I seem to understand lots of things in context and like structure and routine; then I can predict what is going to happen next. I can get upset if I am out of routine.

▓ I am learning that objects can represent real-life activities. For example, I know that my blanket is associated with nap time and that my chair I eat in at home is associated with mealtimes.

▓ I have begun to understand that signs have meaning.

▓ I seem to have started to understand and follow simple routine instructions with a familiar prompt.

▓ I like to communicate. I love intensive interaction and can do this for a long time if you let me lead it. I will smile and laugh when I am really enjoying something.

▓ I use facial expressions and vocalisations to express how I am feeling.

Expressive communication including yes and no, or positive and negative responses:

- I will often clap if I am excited or pleased about something and will push you away if I don't like something.

- I don't like lots of close attention and you need to know me well enough to know when to leave me alone. If I make lots of upset sounds, I might be tired or overstimulated.

- I will request toys and activities by taking myself over to them and reaching towards them. I will do this with the hoist (I love spinning/ walking) and my walker.

- I make choices between toys by reaching for the item that I want.

Yes and no, or positive and negative responses:

- I have a positive response, clapping and smiling.

- My negative response is looking grumpy and pushing you away.

AAC [augmented and alternative communication]:

- My understanding of language is supported by multisensory cues.

- I can make choices using real objects. I struggle to attend to pictures and symbols, so I need real objects to support my understanding and expression.

How to support my communication:

- Use a total communication approach, where all my attempts to communicate are valued.

- I like to have a routine and get excited if things happen that I seem to be expecting. When you change my routine you need to expect me to be a bit unsettled to begin with, but once I have got used to it I will anticipate and participate.

- Use real objects and signing to support my understanding.

- Observe me carefully and follow my lead.

Activity ideas:

- Find things which I like to play with and encourage me to request them.

- Pause motivating activities mid-way and observe my response. Once I have responded, say and sign 'More?' and restart the activity.

160 Focus on Chailey Heritage School

> - Encourage me to follow you rather than push me to the bathroom etc.
> - Intensive interaction
> - Play repetitive 'ready steady go' games to help me anticipate activities.
> - Take turns with a motivating item, e.g. massager, light-up toy. Say ****'s turn . . . my turn' and support him to take turns engaging with the item.
>
> Please see my **Engagement & Sensory Support Profile** for information on **sensory** factors for communication.

Profile 3 – the social and emotional wellbeing profile

Social and emotional and mental health is a section of the EHC Plan which is often lacking. One the authors read recently, for a child who has quadriplegic cerebral palsy and is blind and deaf, had only one outcome, which was for the child to learn that 'things that were hot could be dangerous'. We would argue that developing trusting relationships with the people who were going to take care of him would be the first and most appropriate step for a child who could not move. Again, this needs to lead to a wider discussion about expertise. This profile considers the social and emotional wellbeing of the young person in the belief that without these things they will not be able to learn.

SOCIAL & EMOTIONAL WELLBEING PROFILE FOR ***** TEACHER: ***** SEPTEMBER 2020	
Insert pic here	**Long-term social & emotional wellbeing outcomes from EHC Plan:**
	■ To show intent in interacting with my peers by reaching out to them, leaning my head or offering my feet towards them on a daily basis.

	Long-term social & emotional wellbeing outcomes:
	▓ To be feel happy, secure and understood by the important people in my life
	▓ To continue to develop my decision making in order to maintain my strong sense of independence and self-direction
	▓ To interact with my family and peers in a meaningful way
	Next steps for social & emotional wellbeing:
	▓ **S1** To identify one meaningful item that belongs to me
	▓ **S2** To pass objects to my peers during group sessions with adult support
	▓ **S3** To develop a clear greeting in response to being greeted by a familiar adult

Social Profile:

- ▓ I like familiar people and need the reassurance of a small group of people working with me.
- ▓ When I know you well I will look at you with a cheeky grin, put my feet on you and climb onto your lap for a cuddle.
- ▓ I need to take time out sometimes and will take myself away for a bit of alone time.
- ▓ I like certain children and will move towards them sometimes touching, lying on or holding onto them.
- ▓ It sometimes takes me a while to engage in activities that are not familiar. In order to engage, I need an adult to work with me. I sometimes find it hard to engage alongside an adult when faced with a new activity – I will occasionally cooperate with an adult (allowing you to gently move my hand etc) for around a minute. It helps me if you show me that you are excited to participate too. Once I am interested, I can engage fully and independently for around 5 minutes before I show you that I am finished.

▣ I have become better at noticing where people are in relation to me, and I am better at moving around them rather than crawling over others or self-propelling into them.

Emotional Profile:

▣ I am a good-humoured young man most of the time.
▣ If I am unhappy I might feel unwell, be tired or unsure of what is expected.
▣ I like to have a routine and structure to the day.
▣ I am more accepting of people sharing my space, but I don't always like to be surrounded by people, and if you sit on my sofa, I may try and gently push you off so I can lie down.

How to support my social and emotional wellbeing:

▣ Let me come to you and let me take the lead.
▣ I need to know that you are there to help but won't make me do things.
▣ When it is obvious that I need help, ensure you are within reach so that I can ask for help by grabbing you but don't help immediately. I need to let you know what I want.

Activity ideas:

▣ Intensive interaction
▣ Interaction games
▣ Play alongside me and make yourself interesting
▣ Allow me to be around suitable peers and see what I do.

A real-life example – P

When P started school, she was a tiny curled up ball who would only sit on a lap. She was anxious, jumpy and fearful of any noise. P has quadriplegic cerebral palsy, is registered blind and has severe dystonia as well as severe epilepsy. For her, the world was a noisy, unpredictable and scary place, and she had never left the security of her parents. Her parents were also nervous because her start in life had been difficult and they had nearly lost her several times. P had a jejunostomy (a tube into the jejunum for feeding), but if anyone tried to access it, she would startle, and sometimes, she would accidentally grab it and pull it out. If there was a slight noise in the classroom, her startle reflex would be triggered and she would cry. This would then progress to screaming. We decided that, to begin with, all she needed was to be able to relax in her new environment, get used to the people and develop attachments. Soon she progressed to sitting on the lap of a staff member and then, weeks later, to sitting for several minutes in a wheelchair. We got her used to the noises in the classroom by showing her what they were and then giving a warning using the phrase 'big noise'. Then when she was used to the noise, we removed the warning. Her 'steps' were simple, and she only had a few, which consisted of the things she needed to support her wellbeing and help her relax in the new environment.

Over a period of 2 years, she made wonderful progress, and although she can still be startled by unusual noises, the common noises that can be heard in the classroom are of no concern to her. P's parents also needed care and support as they were very anxious about her settling, and after 6 years at home, they felt that no one would be able to understand her like they did. When they first mentioned this, I told them that this was true but that they could show us how to look after her like they did. This gave them confidence, and as their anxiety and P's slowly disappeared, they discovered that they could have time without her, and it benefited everyone in the family, which ultimately had an impact on P's wellbeing too. As P was left by her parents and we were able to see her personality without the anxiety masking it, we discovered that she had a wonderful sense of humour. This highlights another aspect of what we need to take into account for each of our pupils, and that is personality. Because of what they had been through during P's early life her parents felt anxious and stressed. Part of P's personality was to be anxious, probably made worse by the scary, noisy world she could not see or make sense of.

Profile 5 – a physical profile

It is through motor skills that children learn about the world and become initiators and active participants rather than passive recipients of experience (Kermoian, 1998). As anyone who has been to a long conference knows, sitting still in a chair for a long period is not good for you physically or for your concentration. Neither is it good for young people in wheelchairs. Physical activity is good not only for maintaining health and movement but also for maintaining good levels of engagement. At

Chailey Heritage, everyone does a physical activity every day. Young people who need ventilators have been enabled to use an adapted trike, horse ride and swim. Others who have practised riding their trikes or using walkers for several years have learned to do it themselves.

PHYSICAL PROFILE FOR ***** 2020
Teachers: ***** Named Physiotherapist: *****

	Long-term outcomes:
	▦ To reach my physical potential
	▦ To keep active and maintain my range of movement
	Priority areas to focus on:
	P1 To independently climb down from the class sofa to the floor, demonstrating caution and control
	P2 To purposely move myself across the floor in order to reach a motivating item or person
	P3 To independently make one full rotation of the pedals
	P4 To stand at ladder back for 30 seconds, with minimal support
	P5 To sit on a box for story time, up to 3 minutes, with an adult sitting on the floor beside me (no adult sitting behind me)
	P6 To take steps in the swimming pool with as little support as possible
Current abilities:	**To maintain/progress this skill, I need to:**
Lying down:	
▦ I can lie, roll, go up on my knees briefly.	▦ Have regular opportunities to practise and develop my strength and skills
Sitting:	
▦ I can sit up, move from a sitting to a kneeling position and get myself into all kinds of interesting positions.	▦ To purposely move myself across the floor in order to reach a motivating item or person

Cycling:		
▣ I have a trike and I'm learning how my body moves on it.	▣ To independently make one full rotation of the pedals	
Standing:		
▣ I am now happy to stand in my stander. ▣ I am beginning to stand with you holding me a little at the hips.	▣ To stand at the ladder back for 10 seconds with minimal support	
Walking:		
▣ I can move across the room in the helping-hand sling.		
Vestibular:		
▣ I can sit on the peanut ball with support.	▣ To balance with as little support as possible	
Proprioceptive:		
▣ I can sit on the peanut ball with support.	▣ To lie on my tummy on the peanut ball	
Swimming/hydrotherapy:		
▣ I am happy and relaxed in the water.	▣ To take steps in the swimming pool with as little support as possible	
Rebound therapy:		
▣ I can sit by myself on the trampoline.	▣ To balance myself when someone walks around the trampoline, gently moving me	
Hippotherapy:		
▣ I sometimes try to lie down on the pony.	▣ To sit with minimal support on the pony	

This is A (see Figure 11.3); he is a very intelligent young man and does not have PMLD. He is, however, a very good example of how physical activity and having the opportunity to do what other children can do can have a profound impact on wellbeing and independence. As

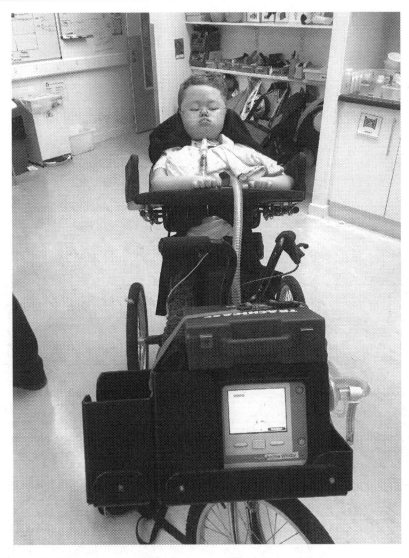

Figure 11.3 A riding his trike

you can see, A is reliant on a ventilator. He also really wanted to ride a bike. He needed an engineer to adapt the bike for his ventilator and numerous occupational therapy and physiotherapy visits to make it possible, but he can now be seen riding his bike, with support, around the grounds. The impact this has had on his physical and emotional wellbeing is huge.

Profile 8 – specific learning profile (profiles 6 and 7 can be found in the next chapter)

This profile includes elements of literacy, numeracy and simple science and becomes more sophisticated as the learner progresses. Not all the young people at Chailey Heritage have one of these, and if they have PMLD, they are very young, or not yet at that stage, they will not have one. If they are learning about reading, numeracy or other aspects of learning not already captured in one of the other profiles it will go in here. The decision was made not to call it a subject-specific profile, as in the wider education world this means something else. Our learners spend a great deal of time working on things which mainstream children do not have to do, such as physiotherapy, occupational therapy and speech and language therapy. Their communication may be slower even though they may understand just as quickly. They may have medical and physical needs which can have an impact on their day and going to the toilet will probably take longer; therefore, they cannot cover as much as mainstream children during a school day.

SPECIFIC LEARNING PROFILE FOR *****	
	Long-term outcomes – EHC Plan:
	▪ To achieve academic qualifications
	▪ To access the national curriculum at an appropriate level
	Long-term outcomes for specific learning:
	▪ To achieve academic qualifications
	▪ To access the national curriculum at an appropriate level

168 Focus on Chailey Heritage School

Literacy Skills: Reading

- I enjoy sharing books and listening to stories.

- I can hear the onset (initial sound) of a familiar word and indicate this by pointing to the right person, photo or object when each option has a different onset.

- I can now also pick out which letters make the sounds in the middle and at the end of words.

- I am able to identify words with the 'ee' sound when given a choice of three words.

- I have been looking at the spellings of words that have an 'ee' digraph in. With support I can identify and spell using, the correct grapheme is 'ee', 'ea' or 'ey'. I would still like to practice this.

- I am gaining confidence at sight-reading familiar names and some other words shown as printed text.

- I like to practise spelling high-frequency words and CVC [consonant–vowel–consonant] words to help me remember them. I also practise finding some words in CCS on my VOCA [voice output communication aids].

Resources:

Library books, Bug Club, Reading Eggs, Grid 3, Chooselt! Maker 3, Visual Timetable, CCS book, Oxford Reading Tree books, Phonic Books, Symbol Talker A, Switchlt! Literacy app, Bug Club books, Collins Connect, Big Cat books

My next steps in reading:

- **R1:** To indicate that where to find the digraphs 'ee','ea','oo','ch','sh' and 'th' in familiar words

- **R2:** To identify the new word when my helper changes the onset of the CVC word

- **R3:** To discriminate consistently between two items starting with different onsets (sounds from Phases 2 and 3 of Letters and Sounds)

- **R4:** To know 5 graphemes from Phase 3 Letters and Sounds

Literacy Skills: Writing

- I can develop a story line with people/objects, a setting and an activity. Please encourage me to use my imagination.

- I can compose simple sentences using familiar words (high-frequency words, CVC words, names). I am able to select a correct word I do this using printed words. I am more accurate when using the plasma screen with a pointer. I listen back to what I have written and can hear if there is, a word missing or words are in the wrong order.

- I can use my VOCA and SuperCore 30 to complete short sentence writing. Using this programme can help me expand the vocabulary I use in my writing so please use my VOCA whenever you can.

- I am able to select the correct letters to complete CVC words

- I am very good at using the correct structure in my sentence (starting with the 'I' pronoun for example).

- My teacher would like me to start using the pronouns he, she and we as this will increase the topics of my writing.

- I can go to the Magic Wand page on my VOCA, and I am learning to explore more types of punctuations and changing words into different tenses.

Resources:

CCS book, words, Grid 3 (touchscreen)

My next steps in writing:

- **W1:** To use the pronouns he, she and we in structured writing lessons with support and prompting

- **W2:** To start to use a wider selection of punctuation in structured writing sessions with support

- **W3:** To use the 'Magic Wand' page on my VOCA in order to change tenses and change a word into its plural form with prompting and support

Mathematical Skills:

- I can confidently identify sets with up to seven objects. I am now working on counting up to eight objects.

- I can confidently identify the next number for numbers up to 20. I am beginning to be more consistent at identifying the next number for numbers up to 50 with support. I would like to continue to work on ordering numbers 0 to 30, and I am becoming more confident in putting the numbers in the correct order and self-correcting myself, e.g. identifying the mistake and correcting it.

- I am interested in exploring numbers on a 100 square, and my teacher feels that I can start to practise looking and naming numbers between 30 and 100.

- I can confidently combine two groups of objects by count the total number of objects (up to 7). I can then identify the correct number on the number line.

- I know if I have too many objects and need to take some away when making sets of up to six objects.

- I am beginning to use the number line with numbers 0 to 10 to subtract. I like to play skittles and find out how many I knocked down by practising counting back on the number line.

- I am beginning to learn to tell the time to the hour.

- I can choose the correct day during the Hello time and know the order of the days of the week.

- I have started to learn to recognise coins and banknotes. I am able to recognise coins from a choice of 2–3 coins.

Resources:

Number cards, lotto, counters, Grid 3, ChooseIt! Maker 3, SwitchIt! Numeracy app, Mathseeds, Espresso.

My next steps in mathematics:

- **M1:** To identify numbers up to 100

- **M2:** To count in 2s using objects and a 100 square

- **M3:** To combine two sets of objects and count the total (within number 10)

> ▨ **M4:** To use objects to take away a small number from any number to 10
>
> ▨ **M5:** To learn to tell the time to the hour
>
> ▨ **M6:** To add a number (0–10) to any number to 10 by counting on using a number line
>
> ▨ **M7:** To subtract a number (0–10) from any number to 10 by counting back on a number line
>
> ▨ **M8:** To learn to recognise coins

All these profiles, as well as those in the next chapter, which also support independence, come together to form the child's personal curriculum, meaning that all the children can fulfil their own potential irrespective of what others are doing. This does not mean, however, that the young people will work in isolation. This is an important point and one which is often asked. The teacher can still teach the young people as a class with the same or similar activities but be working on different steps or skills. The 'Next Steps' are put into a one-page document which is used in the classroom on a daily basis for observation writing.

There are a number of strategies throughout the year which support this system that include the following: different-style lesson observations where the focus is chosen by the teacher to enhance their CPD which is followed by a collaborative discussion with agreed-on outcomes. At the end of each year, teachers have a progress interview with the headteacher and a consultant to discuss the progress of each child in their class. The focus of this is clearly on the teachers' understanding of their pupils and how best to support them. It also includes any barriers to learning the young person may have had that year, for example, operations, illnesses and family issues, amongst other things.

In the classroom, the teacher plans activities which cover the particular 'steps' of the individuals in their class. Each term has a topic through which the activities are derived, even if the skill or 'step' is the same. This keeps it fresh and more interesting for everyone. In times when COVID-19 was not an issue, classes would have regular trips out into the community, and 'steps' would be worked on here too.

Older students would have visits to nearby colleges and socialise with other young people their own age, as well as visits to theatres, libraries, shops, cafes and other schools as well as many other places were common and enhanced skills in real-life contexts.

For those in the UK concerned about what the Office for Standards in Education might think about this system, in October 2019, we presented the CHILD curriculum during an inspection and came out with an 'Outstanding' judgement. We did not present any numerical data at all. What we could do was show the story of progress for any child they chose.

Reference list

Imray, P., & Hinchcliffe, V. (2014). *Curricula for teaching children and young people with severe and profound and multiple learning difficulties; Practical strategies for educational professionals.* London: Routledge.

Kermoian, R. (1998). Locomotor experience facilitates psychological functioning: Implications for assistive mobility for young children. In D. Gray, L. Quatrano, & M. Lieberman (Eds.), *Designing and using assistive technology: The human perspective.* Baltimore: Brookes.

Lacey, P. (2007). Start where the learner is: Coaching for a better quality of life. *PMLD Link, 19*(2), 57.

Supporting independence at Chailey Heritage School

In this chapter, we discuss what independence means for young people at Chailey Heritage and how we go about supporting them to fulfil their potential in this respect. Independence is encouraged in all pupils at different levels, with varying levels of support. The focus is on empowerment: from being able to show they like something and give a positive response to being able to make decisions about their own future, from needing support to do something to being able to do it themselves, from moving one foot a short distance to taking numerous steps in a walker. Support should be as discreet as possible with the focus being on empowering the young person and not on the person giving the support. Staff are trained to facilitate, not to 'do unto'. They are also taught to withdraw support slowly, over a long period, to enhance independence.

Responsive environments

The authors believe that having a voice is fundamental to independence, for all young people with PMLD. As mentioned earlier in the book, we begin with a responsive environment, listening to and acknowledging all communication. After reading Jean Ware's (2003) book *Creating a Responsive Environment for People With Profound and Multiple Learning Difficulties*, we developed a responsive environment in the classroom, and at Chailey Heritage School, it had a profound impact. Tony was a young man in a class a number of years ago. Tony was blind, couldn't blink and needed drops put into his eyes every hour.

He was also deaf and had hearing aids. He was in a wheelchair and could not move any part of his body except an index finger that he could move an inch. He needed suctioning every hour or so as he was unable to swallow, more often when he was not well. Despite all his difficulties, Tony was able to vocalise with different intonations which were understandable to people who knew him well. Because of his complex needs, he had regular visits throughout the day from a nurse, and if they came into the classroom and didn't come to speak to him straight away, he would use an urgent vocalisation which would mean 'come and speak to me'. He could recognise the footsteps of favourite staff and vocalise a greeting. If he needed to be changed or if something was wrong, he had a higher pitched vocalisation. When we sat down as a staff team and looked at all the communication he was showing us, it was striking just how much he was telling us and how much we were responding to instinctively. By responding to him accordingly, it was encouraging him to communicate more often. Despite not having language, movement, eye pointing or any obvious way of communicating, he was clearly expressing a lot and had between 15 and 20 different intonations. Tony had such a large presence in the classroom which is hard to explain to the uninitiated. By the end of his time in my class, we used to joke that Tony was in charge, and I was happy to support that. For someone who had so little control in his life, it seemed right to help him to have any control he could command, and he taught me so much.

When conducting training for staff, I often do an exercise to demonstrate what it feels like without a responsive environment. It consists of getting people into groups of three, sending one person in each group out of the room and telling them quietly that I want them to communicate something they did the previous night to the others in their group. I then tell the groups left in the room that they are to ignore the person returning, not to give them eye contact, not to listen or respond to what they are saying but to completely blank them. When the groups are back together and talking, I observe what happens. I find that some people give up trying to communicate with the group very quickly. They will often sit down, looking dejected and sit and wait for the exercise to finish. Some show some 'challenging behaviour' by climbing on top of others (pre-COVID-19, of course) or clasping the face of others to get their attention by trying to force eye contact. These people are all neurotypical adults who know it is an exercise and yet demonstrate the wide range of behaviour we may see in some of our pupils. After the exercise, I will talk about what I have observed and explore the feelings they experienced. It has a profound effect on many staff, and they often describe feeling 'invisible' or losing confidence, even in such a short time. It is a powerful exercise that I would highly recommend trying with your staff (when it is safe to do so, of course!).

The responsive environment is not only about acknowledging communicative attempts; it is also about expecting and waiting for communication. For example, if a child vocalises, they get attention; this encourages them to vocalise again. They realise that vocalising or moving gains attention and continue to do it, and they often realise they have an impact on the world. So much of what happens to children with PMLD underlines the fact that they have no control of anything in their lives. This is one way in which they can claim back some control. We also use intensive interaction techniques (Hewitt, Firth, Barber, & Harrison, 2011) throughout the day and have times every day when the adults have to be silent and the young people lead the 'chat.' In every

Figure 12.1 J playing with slime

activity, the expectation is that the young person participates in any way they can.

There is a subtle difference between supporting access and supporting participation. To use the example of artwork with a young person. Supporting access could mean that the young person's hand is plonked into the paint and then put onto the paper to make a picture that the young person has not participated in creating. Supporting real participation means helping them to do as much of it by themselves as they can by using hand-under-hand support to feel the paint and then feel the paper by moving their hands independently.

Physical activity

In the previous chapter, we discussed how physical activity has a very important place at Chailey because of the impact on health and wellbeing. It also clearly has an impact on independence. If a young person can begin to roll themselves across the floor or learn to reach out for something that interests them, they are developing their independence. There is another criticism to be made of some Education, Health and Care (EHC) Plans here. When the young person arrives at school, the EHC Plan is often written as if a young person who has physical disabilities does not need to take part in physical activities. In the section 'Sensory and Physical', it often only covers a 'change of position' or is a list of things that the physiotherapist or occupational therapist needs to do and are not outcomes for the young person themselves. That is, of course, if they are lucky enough to have physiotherapy and occupational therapy provision included. We are returning to the question of expertise again.

Each young person at Chailey Heritage does a physical activity every day and there are a range of activities on offer. They can swim in a hydrotherapy pool and do rebound therapy (trampolining) or hippotherapy (riding); many have adapted trikes and walkers, and each classroom has overhead hoists in which the children can use special slings for walking. Each specialist education assistant is trained to assist with these activities, and if you were to wander around the school at any point in the day, you would see all these things going on, even during the lockdowns (more about this later).

Supporting independence **177**

Figure 12.2 L swimming

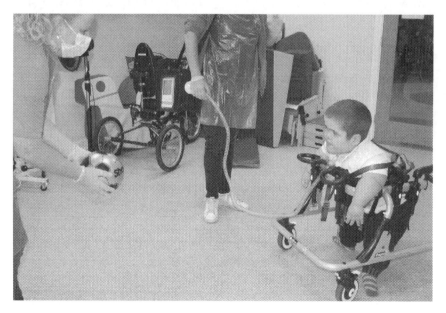

Figure 12.3 L using his walker

Powered driving

Although some young people are able to use walkers or adapted trikes to begin experiencing self-initiated movement, for others, this isn't physically possible, and in many schools, pupils with PMLD who have mobility problems aren't able to experience any self-initiated movement. This suggests that our pupils who cannot move are at a great risk of becoming passive and developing what Miller and Seligman (1975) called learned helplessness. If you cannot physically move yourself, then powered mobility is an option, but for many students, it is often only considered if the likely outcome is that they will become independent drivers and is not considered for the development of engagement and participation in its own right. Hardy (2004) suggests that developmental achievements can occur as a consequence of mobility. Advances in developmental psychology have suggested that the domains of child development (motor, cognitive, language, emotional and social), previously thought of as separate and distinct, are closely intertwined, and an acquisition in one domain can have a positive impact on others. Equally, restriction within a domain can negatively impact the others (Bertenthal & Campos, 1984).

All the young people in our school have opportunities to develop powered driving skills at whatever level they are at. As mentioned, often, children aren't given the opportunity to develop powered driving skills unless they are able to demonstrate that they will become independent drivers. First, how do you develop these skills without practise, and second, this assumes that the only outcome derived from powered driving is to be able to move yourself independently from one place to another.

We strongly believe that a vital part of our job is to encourage our pupils to become active participants rather than passive recipients (Tilbury, 2015). As teachers of young people with PMLD, we spend a great deal of time and effort encouraging participation and supporting the development of contingency awareness. Therefore, *all* our students have access to powered mobility whether they are likely to become independent drivers or not. We have a number of powered bases, designed and built by our research and design engineer, that can fit any wheelchair or buggy onto them, thus giving any young person the opportunity.

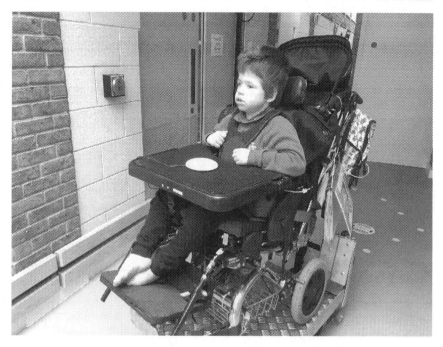

Figure 12.4 J powered driving and testing the acoustics by vocalising

Profile 4 – the access technology profile

Access technology supports independence whilst also enhancing well-being, as young people are able to take control. For some young people, powered driving is on a separate profile, and for others, it is incorporated into the access technology profile. Through access technology, young people can use switches to activate toys, use eye gaze for sensory activities or communication and use iPads or touchscreens to play games and learn.

ACCESS TECHNOLOGY PROFILE ***** July 2020 Teacher: ***** OT: ******	
Pic of young person goes here	Long-term outcomes for access technology from EHC Plan:
	▪ To use technology for independence and play

	Long-term outcome for access technology
	▪ To use access technology to play and for control
	Next steps for access technology:
	▪ To purposefully activate a switch to light up a fibre optic or other light toy and attend to the result
	▪ To press and hold a switch with either of my hands to move a powered platform or activate a switch toy for 30 seconds

Devices I use:

Driving

- ▪ I sit in my own wheelchair on platform 4.
- ▪ I use a single large smoothie switch on a Velcro board on my tray.

How to set up my access:

Driving

- ▪ Make sure I am sitting upright in my chair
- ▪ Attach my Velcro board to my tray to keep the switch in place
- ▪ Position my switch centrally on my tray
- ▪ When I am driving I use my switch to move the powered platform in a turning direction

Switch activities

- ▪ I enjoy toys which give me strong sensory feedback, such as the bells or a vibrating cushion
- ▪ I like to drive on the faster profile 3.

How to support me:

- ▪ Hold the switch in my eye line, before putting it on my tray.
- ▪ Encourage me to press and hold my switch by hand over hand, prompting if I will tolerate it, try 'ready steady. . .' to cue me in.
- ▪ Once I have started to drive, give me the opportunity to drive on my own without intervention.

Supporting independence 181

- Try to have a quiet environment.
- Give me time – I sometimes need to explore the switch and press several times before I take note of the effect I am making.
- If I become preoccupied with bringing my hands to my mouth lift the switch up into my eye line and to my hands to redirect my attention back to the activity.
- I am currently consolidating my understanding of cause and effect using one switch. I am exploring using a small smoothie switch as this will make it easier to introduce a second switch in the future.

Software ideas:
- Help Kidz Learn – cause and effect
- Big bang

Activity Ideas:
- Powered driving
- Switch toys
- Environmental aids with fan, mixer
- Using my switch in the sensory studio for the bubble tube/colour wall
- Using a BigMac to join in 'hello' time and repeated lines in stories, songs and rhymes

E-safety risk assessment:

** is unable to access the internet independently

Profile 6 – a functional skills profile

This covers everything from dressing and undressing, eating and drinking, using the toilet and anything else in which the young person can participate. Participation is a broad concept, and it even encompasses steps such as 'to vocalise when I am ready to be hoisted'.

182 Focus on Chailey Heritage School

FUNCTIONAL SKILLS PROFILE FOR ***** **Teacher: ******	
	Long-term outcomes for functional skills:
	▨ To be as independent as possible

Life Skills:

- ▨ I like to be as independent as possible.
- ▨ I can load my spoon with support
- ▨ I like to choose what I eat.
- ▨ I like to drink with a straw.
- ▨ I can indicate when I have been to the toilet, as well as when I need to go.
- ▨ I like to help with dressing and undressing.
- ▨ I can put my hands, feet out when being dressed to help.
- ▨ I have a wheelchair, which I love to use and need to practise self-propelling in, but should maintain my skill of walking independently.
- ▨ Strategy for toilet – Encourage me to use the 'my PODD' [pragmatic organisation dynamic display] system.

My Next Steps in Life Skills:

- ▨ **F1** –To load my spoon as independently as possible
- ▨ **F2 –** To be able to hold my cup while having my drink with a straw
- ▨ **F3 –** To be able to turn right and left in my wheelchair

Community and Transition:

- ▨ I need to have a familiar routine in order to feel safe and secure. I need to know what is going to happen next and I need to be supported by people who know me and my communication strategies well.
- ▨ I do not like waiting for things but with encouragement, I am able to do this for short periods.

My Next Steps for Community and Transition:

- ▨ To attend to a visual planner so that I develop my understanding of what is going to happen next.

Supporting independence **183**

Figure 12.5 T eating his lunch

Sexuality and PMLD

Sex education is a difficult subject for many concerning young people with PMLD. At Chailey Heritage, we have a specialist PSHE (personal, social and health education) teacher, Helen Dunman, who has put a lot of work and thought into supporting young people and parents in this area, enabling the Foundation to support young people and adults in developing and understanding their sexuality, within the law and safeguarding policies. She has worked closely with SHADA, the Sexual Health and Disability Alliance (SHADA.org.uk). Helen ensured that large mirrors were installed in all changing areas so that students can see the whole of their body when being changed and so develop a greater awareness of their own bodies. She set up a series of sex education sessions for students with PMLD; she has also devised and run projects to enhance disabled young people's positive body image. She has created a personal safety course for older students, aimed at helping empower them in their relationships with others, and created and hosted parent and carer discussion workshops around sexuality and disability, during which parents and carer were able to share ideas and anxieties. Helen has also trained staff in how to talk to children and young people about sensitive areas, such as sexuality, so that questions can be handled appropriately and confidently by staff and that they feel supported in doing this.

Transition post-19

When we are preparing a young person to transition to a future placement, we go through a process of Future Placement Planning (FPP) meetings which aims to ensure the pupil and their families are aware of their options and how they go about pursuing the option most appropriate for them.

Around Year 9, parents are prepared to begin considering future placements. Following the Year 10 review, a number of FPP meetings will be planned to support transition. Appropriate local services, including local authority youth support services, health authority representatives and social services, are invited so that all options can be considered. It allows funding to be applied for and young people to be prepared.

As with everything else at Chailey, this is individual to the pupil and considers their aspirations and abilities. It considers their personality, their interests and what they want to do in the future. It also collates detailed information about their education, health and care from the people who know that young person well. It records detailed information about the young person's preferences such as foods, toothpaste, shower gel or anything else that needs to pass on to a future placement, we call this "independence by proxy" (Yates & Tilbury, 2020). As young people show their likes and dislikes, these are recorded and used to acknowledge what has been expressed.

As with most things, during transition, what can hold us back, is funding. It is disappointing that in 2021, education, for many young people with PMLD, stops, even though the best thing for them would be to continue with their education throughout their lives. Options can be limited, which is why some young people now stay in the 19–30 provision at Chailey.

COVID-19

In the age of the pandemic, it has become much harder to do things in the way we would like. What has been challenging is keeping children

Supporting independence 185

Figure 12.6 A student rock climbing

separated from each other. We would normally get the young people close to each other to develop their social skills which we cannot do whilst keeping them 2 metres apart. Each class is in a 'bubble', but even in that bubble, children have to be kept separate. Intensive interaction is difficult to do while social distancing and deaf children cannot see our mouths in a mask. However, throughout all the lockdowns, the school has remained open, and although many parents have been worried, we have had a good number of children in. Many parents have been grateful that we were able to stay open as caring for some young people is incredibly challenging 24 hours a day 7 days a week. We have all worn full personal protective equipment, which has cost thousands, and morale has remained good. We have had to adapt to the times and keep to our school bubbles. It has led to many complications as the children who need air-generating procedures all need a space of their own, and we have had to be creative in the support of this. A personal curriculum has worked incredibly well in this situation as well as enabling learning to continue at home. All the profiles and My Next Steps documents having been shared with parents, meaning that they can be worked on at home – if parents have the energy, that is. For those parents who have not felt they could send their child in, we have used Teams, the phone and email to keep in touch with pupils and their families.

As we saw in Part II, it is extremely important to support parents as well as the young person themselves. Just listening and understanding their fears or stresses can make a huge difference. Sometimes, a small action by us can make a massive difference to them, especially when they are exhausted.

Independence for young people with PMLD is about looking really carefully and creatively at ways in which they can have control over their own lives. There are many ways in which they will never be independent; however, this does not mean that they have to be dependent in every way. Supporting them to have control, honouring their communication and knowing them well enough to give them opportunities to do the things they like is a start.

Reference list

Bertenthal, B., & Campos, J. (1984). Self-produced locomotion: An organizer of emotional, cognitive and social development in infancy. In K. Barrett, R. Emde, & R. Harmon (Eds.), *Continuities in development*. New York: Plenum.

Hardy, P. (2004). Powered wheelchair mobility: An occupational performance evaluation perspective. *Australian Occupational Therapy Journal*, *52*, 34–42.

Hewitt, D., Firth, G., Barber, M., & Harrison, T. (2011). *The intensive interaction handbook* (1st ed.). London: Sage.

Seligman, M. (1975). *Helplessness: On depression, development and death*. San Fransisco, CA: WH Freeman.

Tilbury, J. (2015). Having wheels means having fun and learning: Developmental achievements can occur as a consequence of mobility. *PMLD Link*, *27*(80), 19.

Ware, J. (2003). *Creating a responsive environment for people with profound and multiple learning difficulties* (2nd ed.). London: David Fulton.

Yates, S., & Tilbury, J. (2020). Independence by proxy. *PMLD Link*, *32*(97), 34.

# Conclusion

This concluding chapter of the book opens up a wider discussion about how society as a whole can promote social justice and support the wellbeing of all by reflecting on the lessons to be drawn from the innovative and outstanding practice in special education described and discussed in the rest of the book. What is desirable for a life lived well not only for those with profound and multiple difficulties (PMLD) but for all of us as well? How can key issues of wellbeing and independence raised in the body of the book be applicable to society as a whole?

We have heard from more than 100 practitioners from all around the world, and we owe them a great debt of thanks, from that first conference at Swiss Cottage School in November 2018 to the closing of the *Lives Lived Well* international survey in July 2020, and if this book has shown us one thing, it is that all over the world, teachers, practitioners and parents are working hard to support the wellbeing and independence of learners with PMLD.

However, although there is much great practice, the authors feel that PMLD teaching is still the 'poor relation' when it comes to education, and the care of people with PMLD is still too far down the list of priorities for education policy makers. The teaching of these young people is undervalued, and as discussed earlier, there is a question to ask about whether senior leadership teams in special education understand the different pedagogy required. There is also insufficient recognition of parents and carers and the impact on them of having a child with PMLD.

We have found that as a society we are perhaps not as socially inclusive as we like to think we are and need to take more responsibility for

DOI: 10.4324/9781003097648-16

each other and especially those with profound learning difficulties. In the UK, Educational, Health and Care (EHC) Plans continuing up to 25 years is a positive development, but they should go beyond 25 to cover the whole life of someone with PMLD. If you have PMLD, you could lose your EHC Plan when you leave school and find yourself going from school to full-time care alongside elderly people who have lived their lives well, whereas yours is really only just beginning. This is an injustice we would like to see change.

There is a real issue with provision after 19 not only in the UK but worldwide. This was, in fact, already highlighted in the report commissioned by the UK Department of Health and written by Dame Christine Lenehan in 2017. She found that the three agencies of Health, Education and Social Care don't talk to each other and that local authorities cannot think strategically, not because they don't want to but because successive funding crises don't allow it. A parent's quote on p. 29 of the report just about sums it up and is widely echoed in the responses to the *Lives Lived Well* surveys:

> I've struggled to get £18,000 for my son in the community. I can't get any more so he is moving to a placement costing £200,000. What happened to the middle?

It will be essential then to oversee provision at post-19 level on a country-by-country basis.

Every child could have for instance a 'wellbeing and independence audit' when they enter their school which is then monitored throughout their school career and beyond into the provision which follows on.

We have also seen that significant barriers exist which stop full participation of the group in the wider community beyond school. We have also seen that policy documents do not always take account of this group because of their tendency to define independence as closely linked to work and independent living, a goal not achievable for those with PMLD as defined in this book. Independence therefore maybe needs to be redefined for this group, but research with and about this group is scarce and difficult to do, and policy is lacking. So how might research develop further in light of the survey findings? The authors suggest that action research be used to examine in detail how wellbeing and independence are enhanced using case studies from around the world and that practitioners, parents and carers be empowered to share what they know instinctively so they can advocate for people with PMLD. Finally, classroom practices as described in Parts II and III should be adopted in the light of the findings in the survey and a network of schools around the world could be developed which can share good practice, techniques and approaches with everyone working in this field.

In our introduction, we promised a 'feel-good' book, and we hope that this is what we have delivered, that readers will get a clear picture of the enormous potential there is for enhancing the wellbeing and independence of this group. We have also seen that society as a whole has a great deal to learn from the approaches we hear about from around the world and that by putting the learner firmly at the centre, rather than imposing some kind of 'one-size-fits-all' curriculum, it is, in fact, the key to a life of wellbeing not only for learners with PMLD but also for everyone and leaves no one behind! We must be clear that the lives of people with PMLD have value and that they deserve to live lives well, not because they can work and pay taxes but because they are members of the same communities as us and of their own. They teach us things we didn't know we needed to learn. As the world gets used to a 'new normal', perhaps there will be room here for a 'new normal' with respect to those with the highest level of need, one in which they are truly acknowledged as people with the same rights to wellbeing and independence and full community engagement as everyone else.

Reference list

Lenehan, C. (2017). *These are our children: A review by Dame Christine Lenehan, director, council for disabled children.* London: Council for Disabled Children.

The *Lives Lived Well* UK questionnaire

Lives Lived Well

A survey about young people in your school with PMLD aged between 14–19.

About a year ago, I asked the delegates at a conference at Swiss Cottage School to write down what they thought the burning questions or issues were around the education of young people with Profound and Multiple Learning Difficulties (PMLD) today. I was overwhelmed by the heartfelt nature of some of the responses. Here are just a few:

- *Capturing their voices: oh, how difficult that is!*

- *I would love to know how all our hard work is followed up once they have left school!*

- *How can we make sure independence isn't just superficial?*

- *I wish we could encourage the local community to engage more with this group.*

- *I just want to make a difference to them and to their family.*

These comments took me back to when I was a teacher of young people with PMLD in schools in Essex and Cambridgeshire. I knew this was the most important sort of teaching I had ever done, but at

190   DOI: 10.4324/9781003097648-17

the same time I was often unable to quantify exactly what I was actually teaching. One Deputy Head later summed up this feeling to me like this: *Some of the most positive things we try to do are the least tangible. You just can't 'measure' them.* We know now that Ofsted's [Office of Standards in Education] Education Inspection Framework (EIF) will take a rounded view of the quality of education schools provide for all their pupils, including those who have profound, complex and multiple needs. Nick Whittaker, Ofsted's Specialist Adviser for SEND [Special Educational Needs and Disabilities], highlighted the importance of this 'rounded view' at the July SEN Policy Research Forum and explained that, in EIF inspections, inspectors will consider how well pupils are prepared for their next steps and their adult lives, including living independently and participating in society. So that is what the *Lives Lived Well* survey is all about. I want to ask schools about their work with young people aged 14–19 with 'Profound and Multiple Learning Difficulties' (PMLD). Why 14–19? Well, because we know from the SEND Code of Practice (2015) that it is from about Year 9 that we have to really start thinking about their future beyond school. In particular, I want to ask schools about their practice in the 'unmeasurables': the things we know schools do so well, but which don't often get recorded. Things like how you support these young people to access the local community, to be as independent as possible, to be happy and comfortable in themselves, and also of course about all the innovative ways you listen to them. In short: This survey aims to find out how schools help these young people to live their lives well: when they are at school and in the future. So, I hope you will take the time to read through the 'Participant Information and Consent' sheet on the next page and then respond to the questionnaire as fully as you can. In March 2020, I will be setting up a chatroom where I will share the findings and also give you the chance to share more of your good practice, ask each other questions or maybe just 'offload'! I will then disseminate the results and share all that good practice so we can all say we have, just maybe, made a difference.

THANK YOU

Andrew Colley

Participant information

This questionnaire is addressed to the person in your school who has oversight of the learners aged 14–19 with 'Profound and Multiple Learning Difficulties' (PMLD). Please pass the questionnaire on to the person you feel is best able to fill it in. **The questions in this survey all refer only to pupils in your school who can be said to have Profound and Multiple Learning Difficulties (PMLD) and are aged between about 14 and 19.** The term Profound and Multiple Learning Difficulties (PMLD) is a fluid and sometimes contested one, and other terms are sometimes used to describe this group. Prior to the recommendations of the Rochford Review (2016) this group may have been assessed at between Levels 1 and 3 or 4 of the National Curriculum P Scales, but they will all normally display the following overriding characteristics to a greater or lesser extent, though not all these characteristics may be present at the same time:

- They will probably be pre- or non-verbal or in other words may not communicate in what we may call 'typical' ways. They may use some words or short phrases but will probably communicate mainly through gesture, body language and behaviour.

- Their direct communication may largely be for needs and wants only.

- They may have a limited understanding of cause and effect and/or object permanence.

- They will almost certainly have difficulty following instructions and may sometimes behave in ways which challenge the people around them.

- Some may also have physical or sensory impairments, medical issues, or use a wheelchair routinely.

- Some may have very severe or complex forms of autism spectrum condition.

- They will require a high level of adult support throughout their lives. The questionnaire should take about 15 minutes to complete and you do not have to answer all the questions.

Should you subsequently at any time decide you do not want your responses being used, you can withdraw simply by emailing the researcher Andrew Colley. Data generated through the survey will be visible only to the researcher. It will be analysed and initially written up as a dissertation in part fulfilment of a Master's by Research at the University of Cambridge, Faculty of Education. It is hoped also that it will subsequently be disseminated through the dedicated chat room, in articles, other publications and at conferences as a valuable resource for everyone involved in the education of young people with PMLD. The questionnaire is anonymous but at the end of the survey you will be asked to give your name and email contact details if (1) You are interested in a follow up interview, either in person by phone or SKYPE, to discuss the issues raised in the questionnaire further. (2) You would like to have access to the 'Lives Lived Well' Chat room which will be open in March 2020 General information about how the University of Cambridge uses personal data can be found at www.information-compliance.admin.cam.ac.uk/data-protection/research-participant-data.

Q1 **Consent** Please tick below to indicate the following:
☐ I confirm that I have read and understand the Participant Information Sheet.
☐ I understand that all personal information will remain confidential.
☐ I understand that data gathered in this study will be stored anonymously and securely.
☐ I understand that my participation is voluntary and that I am free to withdraw at any time without giving a reason.

Please answer as many of the following questions as you can and leave any out which you don't feel able to answer. Please remember that all these questions refer solely to young people in your school aged between 14 and 19 who can be said to have PMLD as defined above. So, for instance, with the exception of Question 3 below about total number of pupils in your school, when terms such as 'learner' 'young people' 'student' etc are used they ALWAYS refer to this group. Thanks.

194 The *Lives Lived Well* UK questionnaire

About your school

Q2 Which of the following best describes your school? You may tick more than one.
- ☐ A Special School
- ☐ A Mainstream Secondary School
- ☐ A special school on the same campus as a Mainstream School
- ☐ A special provision or class within a mainstream school
- ☐ A residential provision
- ☐ Other (please write below)

Q3 About how many pupils are there in your school **in total**?

Q4 About how many pupils are there in your school with PMLD aged 14 or above?

Q5 Does your school have provision for pupils with PMLD beyond the age of 19?

- ○ Yes
- ○ No

Q6 Where is your school?

- ○ Greater London
- ○ South East
- ○ South West
- ○ West Midlands
- ○ North West
- ○ North East
- ○ Yorkshire and Humber
- ○ East Midlands
- ○ East of England
- ○ Wales

The *Lives Lived Well* UK questionnaire **195**

○ Scotland
○ Northern Ireland

Wellbeing

Q7 There are many definitions of 'wellbeing' but if for the purposes of this questionnaire we are defining wellbeing very broadly as **being comfortable, healthy and happy**, can you tell us below in your own words the sorts of things your school does to make sure your pupils with PMLD are comfortable, healthy and happy?

Q8 In what ways does your school try to ensure that your pupils with PMLD continue to be comfortable, healthy and happy once they have left school at age 19 (or 25)?

Q9 On a scale of 1 to 5, with 1 being 'I do not agree' and 5 being 'I completely agree,' to what extent do you agree with Johnson and Walmsley (2010) that many families with a member with PMLD *'live isolated and unfulfilled lives'*.

- ○ I do not agree
- ○ I neither agree nor disagree
- ○ I agree a little
- ○ I mostly agree
- ○ I completely agree

Independence

Q10 Whilst they are at school, in what ways do you encourage or support these young people to be independent? This could include aspects of the curriculum, the social life of the school, resources and facilities, even the architecture or design of the school buildings.

_____

_____

_____

_____

_____

_____

_____

_____

Q11 In what ways does your school try to ensure that your pupils with PMLD continue to be as independent as they can be once they have left school at age 19 (or 25)?

_____

_____

_____

_____

_____

_____

_____

_____

Q12 In what ways does your school ensure that the voice of the learner is central to the process of planning the provision for them whilst they are at school?

_____

_____

_____

_____

_____

_____

_____

_____

Q13 On a scale of 1 to 5, with 1 being 'I do not agree' and 5 being 'I completely agree', to what extent do you believe that a 'proxy' voice such as that of a parent, carer or intervenor can be considered to represent the 'voice' or the 'opinion' of the young person?
- ○ I do not agree
- ○ I neither agree nor disagree
- ○ I agree a little
- ○ I mostly agree
- ○ I completely agree

Q14 Do you have any further comments about Question 13?

_____

_____

_____

_____

_____

_____

_____

_____

Q15 How do you think a young person in this group could be supported to 'develop and express themselves as sexual beings' (Jordan, R, 2014)?

Parents and carers

Q16 Other than at formal events such as Annual Review meetings, parents evening etc, what other opportunities do you have to ensure that the parents of the young people with PMLD in your school are engaged with their child's learning? Tick the **FIVE** which are most common in your school.
- ☐ Whole school activities such as fetes and plays
- ☐ Invitations to visit their child's class
- ☐ Social events in their child's class such as coffee mornings
- ☐ Fundraising events
- ☐ Home visits
- ☐ Through a Family Liaison worker
- ☐ Phone calls
- ☐ Home school communication books
- ☐ Email communication
- ☐ Other _____

Q17 On a scale of 1 to 5, with 1 being 'not at all' and 5 being 'always', to what extent do outcomes described in Section E of an EHC Plan ('outcomes sought for the young person') ever include outcomes for the parents, carers or family too?

The *Lives Lived Well* UK questionnaire **199**

○ Not at all
○ Very occasionally
○ Sometimes
○ Frequently
○ Always

Q18 If you do ever include outcomes for parents, carers or family in the EHC Plan, can you give an example of what an outcome like that might look like?

_____

_____

_____

_____

_____

_____

_____

_____

Community participation

Q19 Of the following elements tick the **FIVE** you feel are most important for ideal or successful Community Participation for this group in their lives both in and out of school, then if you wish add any others in the box below:
☐ Social networks in school
☐ Social networks outside school
☐ Emotional attachments and friendships
☐ Community activities in School
☐ Spending time outdoors
☐ Joining clubs and societies both in and out of school
☐ Having Hobbies
☐ Having a sense of belonging
☐ Being part of a community with other people with PMLD

200 The *Lives Lived Well* UK questionnaire

- ☐ Participation in School Council
- ☐ Participation in the local community
- ☐ A relationship with a carer or personal assistant when that person is not part of the immediate family
- ☐ Other _____

Q20 Are any of the full list above difficult to achieve in practice and why?

_____

_____

_____

_____

_____

_____

_____

_____

Q21 On a scale of 1 to 5, with 1 being 'not at all' and 5 being 'more than,' to what extent do these learners access the community as part of their school provision at the same rate as those with less severe or complex levels of learning difficulty?
- ○ Not at all
- ○ Much less
- ○ Not quite the same amount
- ○ The same amount
- ○ More than

Q22 If 'not at all' or 'much less' why is this, or if they access the community the same amount or even more than those with less complex needs, how is this facilitated by the school?

_____

_____

_____

_____

The *Lives Lived Well* UK questionnaire **201**

_____

_____

_____

_____

Q23 In what ways is the local community able to engage with your PMLD cohort?

- ☐ At school events
- ☐ Informal contact on community trips
- ☐ Visits to the school
- ☐ Contact with other schools
- ☐ At public venues such as swimming pools, theatres etc.
- ☐ On public transport
- ☐ Other _____

Q24 In what ways do you think schools can work to overcome barriers to community participation for this group?

_____

_____

_____

_____

_____

_____

_____

_____

Q25 On a scale of 1 to 5, with 1 being 'I do not agree' and 5 being 'I completely agree,' to what extent do you agree with the statement: *'The social life of someone with PMLD is largely focused on their family or school'*.

- ○ I do not agree
- ○ I agree a little
- ○ I neither agree nor disagree
- ○ I mostly agree
- ○ I completely agree

202 The *Lives Lived Well* UK questionnaire

And one final question!

Q26 To what extent do you feel The SEND Code of Practice takes account of the needs of learners with PMLD aged 14–19 and why?

If you might be interested in taking part in a short interview about the issues raised in this questionnaire either in person by phone or Skype, or if you would like to be sent a link to the chatroom I will be opening in March, or both, please tick to indicate your preferences and add you name and preferred email address in the box underneath.

- ☐ Follow up interview
- ☐ Link to 'Lives Lived Well' chatroom
- ☐ If you have ticked either or both of the above, please add your name and preferred email address in the space below or in the larger box for further comments below. Thank you _____

If you have any comments or further thoughts around the issues raised in this questionnaire, please add them briefly below:

The *Lives Lived Well* international questionnaire

Email text

I have been given your name and email by...

I have been commissioned by educational publisher Routledge to co-author a book with Julie Tilbury entitled: Enhancing Wellbeing and Independence for Young People with Profound and Multiple Learning Difficulties (PMLD): Lives Lived Well. The book will be partly based on the research I undertook recently through Cambridge University on how schools in England support the wellbeing, independence and community participation of this group of learners.

The publishers would like the book to have wider international appeal, so I have devised a short survey for teachers and other practitioners who work or have recently worked with young people with pmld/pimd/polyhandicap in educational or other settings in countries other than the UK.

The link to the questionnaire is below, where you will also find further information:

(LINK)

I would be very grateful if you could complete the question-

naire yourself and/or pass the link on to anyone you know with experience with young people in this group and may be in a position to complete the survey.

THANK YOU
Andrew Colley

Participant Information

The questions in this survey all refer only to young people who can be said to have profound and multiple learning difficulties (PMLD). The term profound and multiple learning difficulties (PMLD) is used in the UK and in some other countries, but other terms are also used to describe this group such as profound intellectual and multiple disabilities (pimd) and polyhandicap. Irrespective of the terminology used, it is possible to say that the people in this group will all normally display the following overriding characteristics to a greater or lesser extent, though not all these characteristics may be present at the same time:

- They will probably be pre- or non-verbal and may not communicate in what we may call 'typical' ways.

- They may use some words or short phrases but will probably communicate mainly through gesture, body language, and behaviour.

- Their direct communication may largely be for needs and wants only.

- They may have a limited understanding of cause and effect and/or object permanence.

- They will almost certainly have difficulty in following instructions and may sometimes behave in ways which challenge the people around them.

- Some may also have physical or sensory impairments, medical issues, or use a wheelchair routinely.

The *Lives Lived Well* international questionnaire **205**

- Some may have very severe or complex forms of autism.

- They will all require a high level of adult support throughout their lives.

If your current or recent practice or experience is not with young people who normally display the characteristics described above, please do not fill in the questionnaire.

The questionnaire is anonymous. However, at the end of the survey there will be the opportunity for you to give your name and a contact email if you are interested in discussing any of the issues raised in more detail with the authors.

The raw data generated will be visible only to the authors, and only the name of the country or geographical region will be referred to in the book *Enhancing Wellbeing and Independence for Young People with Profound and Multiple Learning Difficulties: Lives Lived Well.*

The questionnaire should take about 20 minutes to complete and you do not have to answer all the questions. Should you subsequently at any time decide you do not want your responses being used, you can withdraw simply by emailing Andrew Colley.

Consent

Please tick below to indicate the following:

- ☐ I confirm that I have read and understand the Participant Information Sheet.

- ☐ I understand that all personal information will remain confidential.

- ☐ I understand that data gathered in this study will be stored anonymously and securely.

- ☐ I understand that my participation is voluntary and that I am free to withdraw at any time without giving a reason.

Please answer as many of the following questions as you can and leave any out which you don't feel able to answer. Please remember

The *Lives Lived Well* international questionnaire

that all these questions refer solely to young people who can be said to have PMLD as defined above. So, for instance, when terms such as 'learner', 'young people' etc are used they ALWAYS refer to this group. Thanks

Q1 Which country, state or region do your answers refer to? This could be where you live and work now or have lived and worked recently.

For convenience, in the rest of the questionnaire the term 'your country' will be used when referring to the above.

Q2 How would you describe your professional role or experience with people with PMLD?

Q3 In your country, what sort of educational or other settings do young people with PMLD commonly attend? You may pick more than one.
☐ Special Schools
☐ 'Mainstream' or general school alongside peers with no learning difficulties
☐ Special schools on the same campus as mainstream schools
☐ A special provision or class within a mainstream school
☐ A residential provision
☐ Other (please write below). You may also use this space to provide further details of provision for young people with PMLD in your country.

Q4 In your country, at what age do young people with PMLD tend to leave school and what kind of provision do they tend to go on to after that?

Wellbeing

Q5 There are many definitions of 'wellbeing' but if for the purposes of this questionnaire we are defining wellbeing very broadly as **being comfortable, healthy and happy,** can you tell us below the sorts of things your school or other settings in your country do to make sure young people with PMLD are comfortable, healthy and happy?

The *Lives Lived Well* international questionnaire **207**

_____

_____

_____

_____

_____

_____

_____

_____

_____

_____

Q6 Which of the following is prioritized in your school or setting with respect to young people with PMLD:
- ◯ Their physical comfort
- ◯ Their emotional well being
- ◯ Their physical comfort and emotional wellbeing receive equal attention
- ◯ Other aspects of their wellbeing

Q7 In what ways does your school or setting ensure that pupils with PMLD are involved in the school community?

Q8 On a scale of 1 to 4, with 1 being 'not at all' and 4 being 'more than', to what extent do these young people access the wider community beyond school as part of their educational provision at the same rate as those with less severe or complex levels of learning difficulty?
- ◯ Not at all
- ◯ Less than
- ◯ The same amount
- ◯ More than

Q9 On a scale of 1 to 5, with 1 being 'I do not agree' and 5 being 'I completely agree', to what extent do you think that in your country many families with a member with PMLD live isolated lives.

O I do not agree
O I neither agree nor disagree
O I agree a little
O I mostly agree
O I completely agree

Q10 Generally speaking, is community participation difficult to achieve for people with PMLD in your country and why?

_____

_____

_____

_____

_____

_____

_____

_____

Q11 In what ways do you think schools can work to overcome barriers to community participation for this group?

_____

_____

_____

_____

_____

_____

_____

_____

Independence

Q12. Whilst they are at school, in what ways do you encourage or support these young people to be as independent as possible?

The *Lives Lived Well* international questionnaire **209**

Q13 After they have left school are they able to be more or less independent and why?

Q14 In what ways does your school or provision seek to ensure that the voice of someone with PMLD is heard and that they can express choices and opinions?

Q15 On a scale of 1 to 5, with 1 being 'I do not agree' and 5 being 'I completely agree', to what extent do you believe that a 'proxy' voice such as that of a parent, carer or intervenor can be considered to represent the 'voice' or the 'opinion' of the young person?
- ○ I do not agree
- ○ I neither agree nor disagree
- ○ I agree a little
- ○ I mostly agree
- ○ I completely agree

210 The *Lives Lived Well* international questionnaire

Do you have any comments about the value of a proxy for someone with PMLD?

Q16 What do you think the key 'life skills' a young person with PMLD needs to ensure they can be as independent as possible?

Q17 In your country or region, do you think that learners with PMLD are fully taken into account in educational policy.

If you have any comments or further thoughts around the issues raised in this questionnaire, please add them briefly below:

_____

_____

_____

_____

_____

_____

_____

_____

If you might be interested in talking about any of the issues raised in this questionnaire, please add you name and preferred email address in the box underneath.

Index

Page numbers in *italics* indicate a figure on the corresponding page.

academic curriculum 53
affection, pedagogy of 59, 74
Aiming High for Disabled Children (2007) 30, 31–32
All Our Health Guide 29
alternative and augmentative communication (AAC) 63, 91, 159
Angelman's syndrome 10–11, 141
animal therapy 59
art therapy 59
assessment of child's progress 118, 151
assistive technology 85, 107, 119
augmented and alternative communication (AAC) devices 63, 159
Australia 9, 45, 47, 53, 59, 62, 65, 69, 74, 76, 80, 95, 98, 111, 114, 121, 127, 128, 186, education policy for young people with PMLD 127–130
autism 13, 192, 204

Banerjee, Robin 22
Basale Stimulation 57
belonging 16
best practice, in transition of young people with PMLD 115–116, 148
Bobath Therapy 57
body language: interpretation of 90; listening to 91; *see also* facial expressions
body signing 91
Bryan, Jonathan 156

Capabilities Approach, in acknowledging capabilities of people with learning difficulties 12, 16, 24
capacity, of people with PMLD 23
carers *see* parents and carers
Castle Wood school, Coventry 147
Centro de Día (Day Centre) 112
Centros Ocupacionales (Occupational Centres) 112
Chailey Heritage School, Sussex 39, 52, 86, 120, 130; access technology profile 179–183; advice on writing 'Next Steps' 149–151, 171; approach to caring disabled children 139; assessment 151–152; Chailey Heritage Foundation (CHF) 136; Chailey Heritage Individual Learner Driven (CHILD) Curriculum 39, 141, 144–146, 148, 172; Chailey Heritage Pathways 136; for children with disabilities 135; Class Assessment File of Evidence (CAFÉ) 151; classroom learning 143; communication profile 152, 156–160; COVID-19 pandemic 184–186; 'curriculum' and 'real' learning 146; engagement and sensory support profile 152–155; functional skills profile 181–183; Future Placement Planning

(FPP) 184; Futures Hub, The 136; history of 134–136, *134, 135*; Hub, The 136; Life Skills Centre 136; My Next Steps documents 149–151, 171, 185; nature of a personal curriculum 133; as non-maintained special school 142; physical activity at 176–177; physical profile 163–166; powered driving 178; pupils of 136–139, *137, 138, 140, 145, 156, 166, 175, 177, 179, 183, 185*; real-life example 162–163; responsive environments 173–176; sex education 183–184; social and emotional wellbeing profile 160–162; specialist staff at 139–142; specific learning profile 167–172; subject-specific profile 167; supporting independence at 173–186; supporting wellbeing and independence 143–144; teaching of National Curriculum 146; transition post-19 184
changing places 69
Children and Families Act (2014), UK 30, 36
choice: opportunities for 79–82; pathways for expressing 21–22
Class Assessment File of Evidence (CAFÉ) 151
classroom learning 78, 143
clinical services assessments 148
cognitive skills 112
Colley, Andrew 3, 45, 191–192, 205
communication passports 90, 107, 116
communication skills, development good of 88
community: care 15; concept of 15; definition of 16; ethos, multilayered 62
community participation: barriers to 70; beyond school 65–74; definition of 14; organisational demands for 68; for people with PMLD 13, 16; programmes of 65; and social ties 14; special occasions in 65; and wellbeing 13–17, 35
COVID-19 pandemic 1, 24, 66, 171, 184–186
curriculum: Chailey Heritage Individual Learner Driven (CHILD)

Curriculum 141, 144–146, 148; 'fit for purpose' curriculum 147; 'one-size-fits-all' curriculum 189
Cyprus 1, 47, 57, 63, 72, 111, 129

day-care centres 110
decision-making: engaging parents in 107; for a person with PMLD 22, 92
decline in facilities 106
Delivering Better Outcomes Together consortium 38
Department for Education (DfE), UK 2, 38
dependence/independence, for groups of people with PMLD 23–24, 25
Diagnostic Assessment for the Severely Handicapped 13
dignity 13, 24, 29, 82, 88
disability associations 98
disabled people, sexual selves of 25
Duchenne muscular dystrophy (DMD) 14
Dunman, Helen 183

Early Years Foundations Stage 53
economic utility 36
Educational Health and Care Planning 38
Educational Health and Care (EHC) Plans 84, 119, 123, 148, 176, 188; long-term outcomes for access technology from 159–160; long-term outcomes for attention and concentration from 153; long-term outcomes for communication from 157; social and emotional wellbeing outcomes from 160
educational policy: in Australia 127–130; in Israel 127; in Spain 124–126; educational policy, in England 30–34; *Aiming High for Disabled Children* (2007) 30, 31–32; Chailey Heritage School, Sussex 39, 52; CHILD (Chailey Heritage Individual Learner Driven) curriculum 39; Children and Families Act (2014) 30; National Curriculum 52; *Special Educational Needs and Disability Code of Practice* (2015) 30; *Valuing People Now* Policy Document

(2009) 30–32; *Valuing People* White Paper (2001) 30
educational protocol 123
Education, Health and Care (EHC) Plan 36, 102
Education Inspection Framework (EIF) 37, 190
Elementary Education (1899), UK 14
Emmett Therapies 57
emotional attachments 12, 74
emotional freedom 86
emotional wellbeing 9, 55, 59–60; definition of 60; *Lives Lived Well* surveys on 60; *see also* physical wellbeing
employment 28, 32, 35, 37, 39, 123
empowerment 81
e-safety risk assessment 181
extracurricular activities 112
eye-tracking devices and switches 91

facial expressions 53, 90, 96, 158; *see also* body language
families: with disabled member, isolation *101*; of people with PMLD 64–65; services 108
Finland 47, 51, 54, 61, 72, 76, 111–112, 129
foster homes, private 48, 112
France 2, 47, 54, 129
fun 59, 75, 139, 144, 186
future destinations, after college and into adult life 118–120
Future Placement Planning (FPP) 184

Galdó, María Carrasco 47
General Data Protection Regulations (GDPR) 110
getting to know you, approach for 53–55, 77
Greece 47, 65, 112–113, 128
Guardian, the newspaper 30

happiness: audits 60; hard skill 85, notion of 59
hearing impairment (HI) 150, 154
Hill, Amelia 30
hippotherapy 165, 176
Hungary 47, 52, 73, 77–78, 84, 90, 128
hydrotherapy 57, 119, 165, 176

idiosyncratic signals 23
ignorance of society 70

inclusion 2, 5, 13, 15, 18, 26, 27, 30, 32, 33, 39, 41, 52, 60–62, 65, 70, 72, 125–130
independence, of young people with PMLD: about community participation 199–201; about parents and carers 198–199; at Chailey Heritage School 173–186; common indicator of 36; decision-making skills 92; definitions of 84; developing and expressing 77–79; equality of opportunity 77; expressions of 79, 90; giving opportunities for 'choice' 79–82; gradual reduction of support 78; key indicators of 79; life skills, teaching of 84–86; *Lives Lived Well* surveys on 76, 195–197, 208–210; meaning of 20–21; in personal care 83–84; physical independence 82–83; scaffolding 78; sexual autonomy 87–88; voice, expression of 88–92
India 47, 57, 101, 111, 129
institutional barriers 128
intellectual disability 13
international policy, on wellbeing 28–29, 33, 121
Ireland, *Lives Lived Well* surveys in 45, 47, 60, 65, 72, 111–112, 114, 129
Israel 45, 47, 51, 58–60, 63, 68, 69, 73, 78–80, 82, 89, 90, 91, 94, 96, 111, 114, 121, 127, education policy for young people with PMLD 127

Kenya 45, 47, 73, 78, 111–112, 128
Kimmins, Grace 134–136
Kinaesthetics Therapy 57
knowingness, meaning of 22
knowledge economy 32

Lacey, Penny 147–149, 151
language 59, development of good 36
learners, motivators of 77
life skills, teaching of 78, 83, 84–86
literacy skills: reading 168; writing 169
Lives Lived Well survey 21, 24, 34, 39, 45, 52, 101, 121; about young people in your school with PMLD aged between 14–19, 190–191; about your school

193–194; 'convenience' sampling 124; data generated through 192; on education policies in other countries 124; getting to know you 53–55; on independence of young people with PMLD 76, 195–197, 208–210; international survey 47–48, 56, 61, 76, 111–115; 'Lives Lived Well' Chat room 192; participant information 191–193; on physical wellbeing 55–59, 194–195; questionnaire (2019–2020) 190–202; with respect to wellbeing 50; 'snowball' sampling 124; UK survey 45–46, 55, 87, 93, 105–111, 121–124
Longhorn, Flo 45

Macedonia 47, 111–112, 128
mathematical skills 170
medical/health issues, impacting learning 154
mental health 59–60; definition of 11; and sense of wellbeing 11; of young person with PMLD 11, 60
mental illness: rates of 12; symptoms of 13
micro-communities 15
MOVE programme 57, 82
multisensory impairment (MSI) 148, 150, 153, 154
My Next Steps (MNS) 148, 149–151, 171, 185

National Association of Independent and Non-Maintained Special Schools (NASS) 11
national curriculum 52–53, 127, 146, 192
National Disability Insurance Scheme (NDIS) 112
needs of learners, with PMLD 121–122
New Economics Foundation 29
nonverbal communication 77–78
Norway 47, 71, 73, 76, 81, 83, 92, 111–112, 114, 129
Nussbaum, Martha 12, 21, 24, 33

occupational therapists (OTs) 57–58, 61, 80, 112, 149, 166–167, 176
occupational therapy 57, 112, 166–167, 176
Office for Standards in Education (Ofsted) 39, 136, 172, 190

organisational communication assessment scheme 91
Organisation for Economic Co-operation and Development 28

paid employment, loss of 35, 39
parents and carers: caring for 99–103; EHC Plans 102; experience, of bringing up a child with PMLD 23; involvement in decision-making 107; role of 96; training involving community partners 101; wellbeing of 102
"peer support" for learners, with PMLD 63
people with learning difficulties 32
Perepa, Prithvi 47
personal assistants (PAs) 119
personal, social, health and economic (PSHE) lessons 87
personal and sexual independence 25
personal and social development 34
personal care: assistive technology, use of 85; autonomy of movement 85; coping with stress 86; independence in 83–84; school bathroom/hygiene routines 83; spaces for 69
physical activity, for young people with PMLD 176–177
physical education (PE) 57
physical wellbeing 55–59; daily school provision 55; definition of 60; medical care of young people with PMLD 58; support for 55; see also emotional wellbeing
physiotherapy 56, 117–118, 166–167, 176
Picture Exchange Communication System (PECS) 2, 4
Picture Exchange Systems (PECS) 80
planning for future placement 106
PMLD Core and Essential Standards 123
polyhandicap 2, 204
powered driving, for pupils with PMLD 178
pragmatic organisation dynamic display (PODD) 91, 182
preparatory programmes, for independent life 112
Preparing for Adulthood (PfA) programme 38–39, 123

Index **215**

profound and multiple learning difficulties (PMLD) 1, 13, 45, 191; capacity of people with 23; characteristics of 2; community participation for people with 13, 16, 20; criteria for having 10; decision-making for a person with 22; education of pupils with 4, 9; Essential Service Standards 37–38; parents and carers of children with 14; parents' experience of bringing up a child with 23; "peer support" for learners with 63; *PMLD Link Magazine* 45; right of young people with 25; sexual autonomy of people with 30; teaching young people with 4

profound intellectual and multiple disabilities (PIMD) 2, 9, 204

proxy voice, issue of 92–99, *93, 94*

public attitudes, towards people with PMLD 70

Public Health England 29–30

public services, for wheelchair users 69

quadriplegic cerebral palsy 160, 162

quality of life 9, 13, 29, 128

Rebound Therapy 57, 165, 176

reflexology 57

residential schools 58, 63, 66, 83, 106–107, 112

respiratory therapies 58

responsive environments, for young people with PMLD 173–176

Rett's syndrome 141

risk assessments 63, 68, 181

Rochford Review (2016) 192

scaffolding 78

School Census Statistics (DfE) 3

school: community, participation in 60–65; practice, for wellbeing 51–53; provision, for young people with PMLD 111

self-care, management of 25, 35

self-fulfilment, feeling of 52, 103

self-help skills 102

Sen, Amartya 12

sensory activities, ideas for 155, 179

severe learning difficulties (SLD) 2, 10, 14, 129–130

severe profound and multiple learning difficulties (SPMLD) 147, 149

sex: education 25, 183–184; fundamental right to 30

sex and relationship education (SRE) lessons 87

sexual autonomy, of people with PMLD 30, 87–88

Sexual Health and Disability Alliance (SHADA) 183

sexualised behaviour, by young learners with PMLD 25

Singapore 47, 51, 54, 56, 58, 60, 62–63, 65–66, 69, 77, 82, 92, 97, 100–111, 113

skills: to keep a young person safe 118; nurturing set of 116–117

Slovakia 47, 98, 128

snoozland therapy 59

social and emotional wellbeing 39, 107, 160, 162

social and family ties, fragmentation of 15

social distancing 185

socialisation, opportunity for 63

socially isolated people 15

social networks 74; in COVID-19 lockdowns 14; impact on wellbeing 14; quality and shape of 24; as sources of emotional support 15

social participation 86

social services 81, 100, 128, 184

social skills 86, 185

social ties 14

soft skills, types of 85

Spain, education policy for young people with PMLD 47–48, 51–52, 54, 57, 59, 61–62, 68, 71, 76, 80, 93, 94, 97–98, 101, 111, 114, 124–126; inclusive education policy 125; *Lives Lived Well* survey 124; *Plena inclusion* movement 125

Special Developmental Schools 127

special educational needs (SEN) 36, 73, 87, 112, 146

Special Educational Needs and Disability Code of Practice (2015) 30, 34–37, 46, 53, 92, 106, 121, 190–191; guidance in 123; implications of 123; with relation to learners with PMLD 122

special schools ii, 3, 11, 18, 27, 37, 46, 48, 53, 62, 63, 70–73, 122, 125,

128, 136, 139, 141, 142, 146, 147, 148, 206
specific, measurable, achievable, realistic, time-limited (SMART) targets 34, 123
speech and language therapist (SaLT) 47, 82, 113, 124, 149, 157
speech therapy 91, 112
Steiner School, Hungary 78, 84, 90
Steiner/Waldorf School, Hungary 52
Stiglitz Report (2009) 29
stimulus, response to 91
stress, coping with 86
structured leisure activities 112
students, tracking progress of 120, 151
subjective wellbeing, theory of 9
supported living 119–120
Swiss Cottage School, London 45, 187, 190
symbolic communication systems 2

Taiwan 47, 78, 113, 129
talking therapy 11
teaching assistants (TAs) 58
teaching, to help PMLD students: ethos of 76; sense of joy and satisfaction 77; in Singapore and Thailand 77
Thailand 47, 51, 60, 62, 65, 73, 76–78, 82, 96, 112, 128
Timor Leste 47, 95, 128
total communication 91, 159
transferable skills, importance of 78
Transición para la Vida Adulta (Transition to Adult Life Centre) 112
Transition Officer 106, 110
transition, of young people with PMLD: from child services to adult services 116–117; good practice in terms of school/college collaboration in 115–116; issues faced during 116–117; planning for 108

United Kingdom (UK): Children and Families Act (2014) 30; Department for Education (DfE) 38; Department of Health (DoH) 30; educational policy in 30–34; Electoral Commission 33; government policy on wellbeing 29–30; residential schools in 106–107; *Special Educational Needs and Disability Code of*

Practice (2015) 30; Wellbeing Manifesto for a Flourishing Society 29
United Nations (UN): Children's Fund 29; Convention on the Rights of Persons with Disabilities (2007) 29; Convention on the Rights of the Child (1989) 29; General Assembly 28; Stiglitz Report (2009) 29
United States (US) 47, 69, 80, 111, 128–129

Vagal Nerve Stimulator (VNS) 154
Valuing People Now Policy Document (2009) 30–32
Valuing People White Paper (2001) 30
verbal communication 32, 97
video transition package 107
visual impairment (VI) 150, 157
vocation 117
voice, of young person with PMLD 89, 91–92, 95, 97, 115, 173
voice output communication aids (VOCAS) 91, 168

Ware, Jean 173
warmwater therapy pools 57
wellbeing: adopted by schools 51; community participation and 13–17; definition of 10–11, 28, 50; individualised approaches to 51; meaning of 9–13; repositioning of 55; of young people with all learning difficulties 10
Wellbeing Manifesto for a Flourishing Society 29
wheelchairs, use of 69
World Bank 128
World Fit for Children, A (2002) 29
World Health Organisation (WHO) 28

Yates, Simon 147
young people, with PMLD: capacity of 23; community participation for 13, 16, 20; education of 4, 9; equality of opportunity for 77; medical care for 58; moving from child to adult services 116–117; right of 25; schools, access in 56, 64, 66–67; use of wheelchairs 69; voice of 89, 91–92, 95, 97, 115

Printed in the United States
by Baker & Taylor Publisher Services